LIVERPOOL
THE GLORY
DECADE
1980 IAN ST JOHN **1990**

LIVERPOOL
THE GLORY
DECADE
1980 IAN ST JOHN 1990

First published in Great Britain in 1990 by Sidgwick & Jackson Limited

© Copyright 1990 Brown Packaging Limited, 257 Liverpool Road, London N1 1LX

ISBN 0-283-06058-1

Printed in Great Britain by Severn Valley Press, St. Ives Group, for Sidgwick & Jackson Limited, 1 Tavistock Chambers, Bloomsbury Way, London WC1A 2SG

ACKNOWLEDGEMENTS

The quotations by Ray Houghton on pages 28, 33, 88 and 94 are from *Ray Houghton's Liverpool Diary*, published by Queen Anne/Macdonald.

The quotations by Alan Hansen on pages 28 and 80 are from *Tall, Dark and Hansen*, Alan Hansen and Ken Gallacher, published by Mainstream Publishing

The quotations by John Aldridge on pages 29 and 30 are from *Inside Anfield*, John Aldridge with Brian Woolnough, published by Mainstream Publishing

The quotations by Rogan Taylor on pages 100, 102 and by Kenny Dalglish on page 110 are from *Out Of His Skin – The John Barnes Phenomenon*, Dave Hill, published by Faber and Faber

The quotations by Kevin Keegan on pages 61 and 64 are from *Kevin Keegan – An Autobiography*, published by Arthur Barker Ltd

The quotation by Sammy Lee on page 27 is from *From Schoolboy To Superstar*, Patrick Barclay, published by Puffin Books

We thank the publishers for permission to quote from the above works. If we have inadvertently not credited any other sources then we should like to apologise.

PICTURE ACKNOWLEDGEMENTS

Allsport: Pages 10, 11, 12, 13, 55, 61(bottom), 87, 97, 98, 101, 103 (bottom), 116, 117.
Associated Sports Photography: Pages 19, 22.
John Cocks: Pages 60 (centre), 61 (right), 63.
Colorsport: Front and back cover, pages 7, 8, 16, 18, 20, 21, 23, 24, 25, 26, 28, 31, 32, 34, 35, 36, 38, 41, 42, 44-45, 46, 47, 48, 51, 53, 56, 57, 60 (top), 62, 67, 68, 69, 70, 71, 72, 74, 77, 78, 79, 80, 81, 82-83, 89, 90, 91, 94 (top), 102, 104, 106, 107, 108, 109, 111, 112 (top, bottom and centre).
Empics: Page 29.
John Frost Newspaper Service: Pages 92-93.
Professional Sport: 114, 115.
Sporting Pictures: Page 2, 15, 94-95 (centre), 95 (bottom).
Bob Thomas Sports Photography: Pages 50, 58, 64, 65 (top & bottom), 82 (left), 83 (right), 85, 86, 113 (top & bottom).

Front cover: Alan Hansen and Jim Beglin parade the FA Cup around Wembley after the Cup Final victory of May 1986.

CONTENTS

PREFACE

The greatest experiences of my playing life were with Liverpool Football Club, and like all former Liverpool players I am proud to have been part of something that has become such a symbol of footballing excellence. I hope this book gives an accurate impression of the club over the past decade — a decade of unprecedented success and great football.

Collecting the information and material for this book has been an enormous task, and I should like to thank the various contributors: John and Leo Moynihan for their work on the early years of the decade; Stan Liversedge for the material on the double triumph; Tim Stanley-Clamp for the information on running the club; Stephen Kelly for the fans and the managers; and David Prole for the monumental task of compiling the statistics.

Many people within the game and the club itself have helped with insights and information: I should like to thank especially Kevin MacDonald, John Aldridge, Bobby Robson and Arsenal manager George Graham. Finally, I should like to thank Martin Chilton and Ashley Brown for their efforts in writing, editing and producing the final manuscript.

Opposite: Coming on to the pitch towards the end of my time at Anfield – when Everton fans used to sing 'We hate Bill Shankly, we hate Big Ron, but most of all we hate St John...'

GOING BACK TO SHANKS...

The Liverpool of today is in direct line of descent from the Liverpool sides that were set up by Bill Shankly, one of the most influential football managers there has ever been. Shankly took the club to the top, and set up a system that has kept it there ever since

Bill Shankly was formally appointed manager of Liverpool Football Club on Tuesday 1 December 1960 after a Board meeting that was as important as any that has ever taken place in the history of the club. For there is a straight, unbroken line from his period in charge to the present run of success. Since that December day, the club has had to make many decisions, and, although not all of them have been correct, the big decisions have all been spot on. A style of play, management and direction has been developed that has proved more effective than anything seen before in the Football League. But before looking at the phenomenal side of the 1980s, it is essential to see just what it grew out of, and the traditions it relies on.

The Liverpool Football Club that Shankly joined was a Second-Division side, and had been for six years. But Liverpool FC had a long and distinguished history. It had been founded in May 1892, the result of a split between the owner of the Anfield ground and Everton, the club that used the ground. Everton moved away to Goodison, while businessman John Houlding, the ground owner, established his own side, a side that played its first game in September 1892, in the Lancashire Football Association League.

Scottish connections and an early promotion

The side that played this first game was composed entirely of Scots, recruited by John McKenna, a dynamic character who ran these early sides. This Scottish connection was to prove a lasting strength in the club's history. In September 1893, McKenna's team played in the Second Division, and gained promotion after a

Bill Shankly, one of the greatest motivators that the game of football has ever known, and one of the most knowledgeable of managers. The combination of enthusiasm and knowledge was overpowering.

season in which they were unbeaten. They were now a force in the land, and in the pre-war period notched up some noteable feats — in the 1895-96 season, gaining promotion from the Second Division again they scored 106 goals and they won the First Division Championship in the 1900-01 and 1905-06 seasons. They first used their famous red strip in the 1898-99 season (previously, colours had been blue and white quarters).

Paisley, Stubbins and the great Billy Liddell

In the inter-war period, there was further success, with two League Division One titles in successive years, in the 1921-22 and 1922-23 seasons and the club was not relegated, although it suffered some poor seasons in the 1930s. Then came further glory after the Second World War was over. The Club won the First Division Championship in the first full season of football, 1946-47. This side had consistency in defence (and, in fact, two of the half-backs, Bob Paisley and Phil Taylor would go on the manage the club) but its greatest strengths lay in attack, featuring Jack Balmer (who scored three successive hat-tricks in League games during this season), former Newcastle United star Albert Stubbins at centre-forward and the great Billy Liddell on the left wing.

Liddell was a big Scot, who had joined the club in 1938. His sheer power and speed unnerved defences, while he had a savage shot. Liddell's greatness shone out as the club's results got poorer during the late 1940s, and although there was an FA Cup Final appearance in 1950 (the Club lost 2-0 to Arsenal) the slide continued until Liverpool were relegated in 1954.

Under former player Phil Taylor as manager, Liverpool looked a good Second Division side — challenging for promotion in all seasons from 1955-56 on. But in spite of good members of the side — inside forward Jimmy Melia, winger Alan A'Court and full-back Ronnie Moran — the club never quite achieved promotion, twice

finishing fourth and twice finishing third. By the beginning of the 1959-60 season, the Board were looking for a successor to Taylor, who was himself wearying of the battle, and the Directors had their eye on a Scot across the Pennines. Bill Shankly was then managing Huddersfield Town, where he was developing a side that included two players who were already seen to have big futures, and were to develop into world class in the 1960s — Denis Law and Ray Wilson. Huddersfield had beaten Liverpool 5-0 the previous season, and Liverpool Directors met the pugnacious, confident Scot in November 1959. He agreed to join Liverpool once Taylor had resigned, and in his last game in charge of Huddersfield, on 28 November, his side beat Liverpool 1-0. Three days later, the Liverpool Directors met to confirm the new appointment.

'Liverpool was a city of a million people with a deep love for football'

Shankly had had a typical background for a footballer, coming from a large mining family in Ayrshire. There were 10 children, and the five boys all became professional footballers. In those days, there was the pit or there was football, and precious little other choice. If you had the talent, it had to be football. His career, as a mobile wing-half, was more successful than most — he played for Scotland and won an FA Cup

Right-winger Ian Callaghan on the ball, while Scots imports Ron Yeats and a certain Ian St John wait to see what he'll do with it. Callaghan was not a flyer; as a winger – we were instructed to go over and play one-twos with Ian when he had the ball. He was a great servant of the club, still playing in the triumphant European Cup Final of 1977.

Winner's Medal for Preston in 1938. He ended his playing career with three seasons for Preston after the war, and then went into management, with Carlisle, Grimsby, Workington and finally Huddersfield.

Shankly made it clear that he came to Liverpool because he thought it was a big club that could go a long way. As he told the City's newspaper, the *Liverpool Echo*: 'I could sense the potential among the crowd, the people who wanted to see their team back in the First Division. They were desperate for success and it was all there ready to be directed. Liverpool was a city of a million people with a deep love for football. The potential was tremendous and that is why I came to Anfield.'

Shankly certainly came to represent something to the fans as no manager had done before. Probably his greatest gift to the modern club is how he established a tradition of honesty, enthusiasm and a conviction that the need of the fans for a successful team had to come before everything else. His sayings are still repeated throughout the Football League as examples of football wisdom — given their force by the fact that the great man himself uttered them.

When Shankly joined Liverpool, he told the coaching staff — at that time Reuben Bennett, Bob Paisley, Joe Fagan and Albert Shelley — that he would leave them in their present jobs provided they implemented his own training policy. As Paisley said later: 'He did the sensible thing at Liverpool by getting to know the training group and and seeing who was looking after the reserves. He said he liked what he saw and asked us all if we would stay. We jumped at it!'

Paying the money and getting the right players

This shrewdness extended to the playing staff, for although 24 players left Anfield in the two years after he took over as he rebuilt the team, few of the real prospects were let slip. Shankly got his coaching staff

Left-winger Peter Thompson could take any full-back on and expect to beat him. Shankly would say, 'Isolate Peter, let him beat one or two men.' But he did more than his his fair share of supporting the defence. It was a privilege to play alongside Thompson and Callaghan.

and the apprentices cleaning up the Melwood training ground and repairing Anfield itself — there was the appearance and feel of change, but the baby was certainly not thrown out with the bathwater.

But it wasn't only the Liverpool manager who made the right early decisions. The Board too, partly under the influence of new Director Eric Sawyers, and partly under the stewardship of Chairman TV Williams, allowed Bill his head where critical transfers were concerned. Shankly made some reasonably priced purchases, such as getting Gordon Milne from Preston for £12,000 in 1960, but the club finished in third place in the Second Division in both 1960 and 1961. Shankly decided he had to spend more money — and in two cases he was allowed to. The first was critical to me: he brought me down from Motherwell for £37,500 — the other was when he bought Ron Yeats from Dundee United for £30,000.

The team that Shanks set up in that season stormed to the Second Division Championship, and then became one of the leading sides in the country during the rest of the 1960s. It won the First Division title in the 1963-64 and 1965-66 seasons, and took the FA Cup in 1965. For the rest of the decade it was always one of the hardest sides to beat.

So just what did Shankly bring to the team? First of all, there was his enthusiasm. He radiated confidence

Tommy Smith, sometimes known as the Iron Man. He was a winner, who hated to be beaten. He became an important driving force in Shankly's team, and led the side by example. He didn't need to be dirty in his early years, because he tackled so hard anyway. 'Go in and shake his bones, Tommy,' would be Bill Shankly's instructions before a game.

sign for Shanks if he had set his mind on getting you, because you knew that he was not shamming, not joking when he talked about how great a future a player could have with Liverpool. He believed it, he could see how he was going to achieve it, and so did the player.

But Shankly not only inspired his players, he also inspired the fans. He had the gift of finding a phrase that might exaggerate, but expressed something that thousands of supporters could identify with. He was a natural communicator, who instinctively said and did the right thing in public. And the reason he said and did the right thing was because he felt a great affinity for the fans, and realised that they were the basis of what he was trying to build.

'It made me feel scared, looking at those men with so much experience'

This deep interest and feel for the game, going back over decades, has remained a key part of the Liverpool set up to the present day. Terry Neil, former manager of Arsenal, once described what it felt like looking at the Liverpool bench when he took the London club to Anfield in the late 1970s: 'It made me feel scared, looking at those men with so much experience and enthusiasm for the game. Bob Paisley had been playing before I was born...They knew so much.'

The second part of the Shankly legacy was the way he established a way of doing things that has not been abandoned even to this day. In 1981, Craig Johnston recalls going to the training ground at Melwood and wearing tracksuit trousers — he was told in no uncertain terms that even though it was a freezing cold day, he would train only in shorts, because that was the way it had been done since the days of Shankly. Small rituals, in which everyone has their allotted place, may seem silly to outsiders, but they have fostered an attitude that gives the squad great strength. Perhaps the most important part of this is that no-one — absolutely no-one — is bigger than the ritual, and by extension cannot be bigger than the club. Very few other major clubs have been able to impose this attitude.

'Never pass the ball to one red shirt if there's two in another direction'

Thirdly, Shanks developed a style of play that has basically been the style the club has used ever since. He was insistent that his players keep possession and not give the ball away — 'Never pass the ball to one red shirt if there are two in another direction,' was an instruction he would drum into us time and time again. But this possession football wasn't just a way of avoiding defeat, or of slowing the game down. Liverpool teams swarmed at the opposition, keeping up the pressure, always looking for openings. In the mid-1960s side, there were two wingers — Ian Callaghan and the

and conviction, and made every Liverpool player feel that he was part of a great club. But the confidence he inspired was not just blind faith. He was so convincing because his knowledge of the game was so deep. He made it his business to find out as much as he could about the game of football, and impressed everyone with the information and insights he had on tap. He could walk into a room and dominate a conversation about the game because he had absorbed so much more than other managers about the details that make up any match. To players — and to young players especially — his memory for games, players and incidents could appear uncanny. It was difficult not to flying Peter Thompson — always looking for the chance to break through rather than to defend. We could do this partly because we were very fit — maybe the fittest team in the country at the time — but also because Shankly, perhaps more than any other manager, understood football as a team game.

The period when a team would have one or two big stars, whom they would look to to win games (as previous Liverpool teams had looked to Billy Liddell) was changing. Tactics were moving on and the whole side had a critical balance that had to be adjusted if the results were to keep coming in an era of the new formations (4-2-4 or 4-3-3, for example) that had replaced the old W-M of the 1950s Football League. Teams such as Manchester United and Spurs, successful though they were in the 1960s, represented the other direction. The other team that was really showing the way that football would go was Don Revie's Leeds United, and in the late 1960s and early 1970s, you'd have to say that Leeds, with a younger side and some great talents moulded together by Don Revie, were more successful than Liverpool. But Shankly's fourth, and perhaps greatest gift, to Liverpool came in the early 1970s. He had set up a way of playing that led to success; now he and his staff managed to find a way of changing one successful team so that it gradually developed into another successful team — perhaps the most difficult job in football management.

Shankly had been buying new players to replace his 1960s stars during the decade itself, but none, apart from that human dynamo Emlyn Hughes, had really made the grade. Then, suddenly it seemed, a new Liverpool team was in place by the 1970-71 season, featuring Ray Clemence in goal, a new centre half in Larry Lloyd, a new centre forward in John Toshack and a flying young winger in Steve Heighway. These new faces were grafted on to a solid core of experience in the shape of winger turned midfielder Ian Callaghan, full-back Chris Lawler and rock-hard defender Tommy Smith. This side reached the FA Cup Final in 1971, where it was beaten 1-2 by double winners Arsenal.

Shankly's new team – Kevin Keegan joins the club

After this game, when the team returned to Liverpool, Shankly addressed the crowds who responded enthusiastically to the team: 'At Wembley we lost the Cup. But you, the people, have won everything...I have always drummed into my players that they are playing for you, the greatest public.' And just before the Cup Final itself, he had signed for the club a young player who was the catalyst that turned this team into a great side and forged a magnificent rapport with this public: former Scunthorpe forward Kevin Keegan.

This new-look Liverpool took the League title in 1973, and won the UEFA Cup, Liverpool's first European trophy, that year. Shankly's second great side was

distinctly different from his first, 1960s, model. For a start, it relied more on a squad system than a settled first team. Having to play in the League, in European competition, in the FA Cup and the League Cup put more wear and tear on players than had ever been seen before, and so there had to be players who could be slotted in, and do the job properly, while others were resting. But retaining possession was still at the core of Liverpool's play — as they showed in the FA Cup Final of 1974.

'...the finest performance any team has given in a Wembley Final'

That Cup Final was a real test for Liverpool, facing a strong Newcastle United side that had a fine Cup tradition and boasted an excellent centre-forward in Malcolm Macdonald. Liverpool's stopper centre-half Larry Lloyd was absent (he had been injured earlier in the season) and there were fears about how the defence would hold up. In the event, however, Liverpool put up a majestic performance and ran out easy winners, 3-0, and the threat of the old-fashioned centre-forward was snuffed out by a raw young defender, Phil

Roger Hunt, was a great worker up front, and no-one could wish for a better striking partner. We could create space for each other – 'Take the centre half for a walk,' Bill Shankly would tell me, and Roger could exploit the space. Hunt had skill in both feet and could shoot from anywhere in the penalty area.

Thompson. Shankly said: 'That could have been the finest performance any team has given in a Wembley Final.'

What was so impressive about the victory was the way it was achieved. The style of play, passing the ball about immaculately and running hard off the ball to create space, was an object lesson in how football could, and should, be played at the highest level, where the skills of the individual were put at the disposal of the team as a whole. Skills were there in abundance, but sometimes coming from unexpected quarters: full-back Alec Lindsay was a stylish player coming forward, with an immaculate pass, while Peter Cormack in midfield had beautiful instant control — perhaps better than the control of the more famous forwards Keegan or Steve Heighway.

The great display at this Cup Final was Shankly's last triumph. He had decided to retire, and the announcement was made on 12 July 1974. His successor, announced later that month, was to be Bob Paisley, his assistant manager and one of the coaching staff Shankly had decided to keep on when he joined in 1960.

The appointment of Bob Paisley as manager

The decision to appoint Paisley, rather than to go for someone with a proven record of previous success as manager in his own right, was absolutely correct, and showed that the Board had understood precisely what Shankly had managed to achieve. To bring in someone from outside would have risked upsetting the balance of a machine that was humming along fine — and the machine was not dependent on just one player or indeed any one individual. Bill Shankly had done what few men ever manage: he had set up something — call it a system, an organisation or whatever — that could survive him and be moulded by others into something that changed with the times but yet never lost its essential strength.

Survive Shankly the system certainly did, for the great man himself died in September 1981, at the very beginning of Liverpool's unprecedented decade of success.

Bill Shankly had had one major weakness as a manager: he had always been uncomfortable when travelling, especially when flying, and he had an obscure feeling that somehow, somewhere, events would conspire against his teams when they played abroad. He had almost laid this ghost to rest when Liverpool won the UEFA Cup in 1973, but this was the least important of the European competitions. Under his successor, Liverpool were to rise to a position where they were the most feared club team in the Continent.

In Bob Paisley's first season in charge, Liverpool came second in the League — and Paisley, the most

successful manager that the British game has ever known, has since confessed that he saw this as something of a failure. But the next season his team won both the League Championship and the UEFA Cup — as Shankly's men had done three years before. The following season, 1976-77, the side looked just as good. By now, it had changed yet again from the team of the early 1970s, but suffered no hiccups of form as its forward line of Toshack, Keegan and Heighway was supported by a new midfield featuring Ray Kennedy, Terry McDermott and Jimmy Case.

One night in Rome – winning the European Cup

In 1977, Liverpool made the transition from being the best team in the Football League (they won the League title that spring and were beaten finalists in the FA Cup) to being the best team in Europe, for they won the European Cup, the premier prize in world club football, in a thrilling final in Rome, against Borussia Moenchengladbach. The game marked a decisive shift in the power basis of European soccer, because the German sides that had dominated in the mid-1970s were now on the decline, and it was the Football League that was to take the initiative for the next eight years.

That night in Rome, all the lessons that Shankly had laboured to instil into his teams were put into practice by Bob Paisley's great side. Midfielder Terry McDermott scored the first goal, and covered acres of ground as he chased and harried the Germans; veteran Tommy Smith proved a solid rock in defence, and popped up in the German penalty area to score the second goal, while Kevin Keegan led Bertie Vogts — thought to be the best man-to-man marker in Europe — a merry dance, until Vogts brought him down in the penalty area and Phil Neal stroked home the penalty.

Exit Kevin Keegan – enter Kenny Dalglish

This victory was the more gratifying in that it took place just a few days after after Liverpool lost the FA Cup Final to Tommy Docherty's Manchester United. Paisley managed to raise his men for a supreme effort, and they did not let him down.

This match in Rome was Kevin Keegan's last for the club — having announced that he would be leaving Liverpool to look for new challenges abroad he had signed for PSV Hamburg. There were two other veterans in the Liverpool side that took the Cup whose careers with the club would not last much longer — Tommy Smith (who had scored that vital second goal) and Ian Callaghan.

Having won the European Cup in 1977, Paisley's team then retained it against Bruges at Wembley in

1978, with a side that seemed very different to the one that had walked on to the pitch in Rome the year before. There were three significant new players: up front, Kevin Keegan had been replaced by Kenny Dalglish; in midfield, Ian Callaghan's number 11 shirt was worn by Graeme Souness; and at the back, a young Scots defender, Alan Hansen, was making an early appearance. These three men would be the backbone of the side that swept Liverpool Football Club into the early 1980s.

1978-79 – the meanest defensive record in the Football League

Paisley was already setting a new 'rule' for Anfield — always try to replace a player with someone who is just that bit better. Dalglish slotted effortlessly into the side and proved a more all-round influence than Keegan;

Emlyn Hughes exchanges pennants with Borussia captain Bertie Vogts before the 1977 European Cup Final, the game that saw Liverpool step up a level in world rankings. Hughes could play at full-back or in midfield, but by this time was a central defender where his pace was invaluable.

Souness was the complete midfield player, and Alan Hansen brought a new dimension — genuine class and composure on the ball — to playing the ball out from defensive positions.

Liverpool took the League title for the 1978-79 season and established a record by conceding only 16 goals in the competition. They had won this Championship five times in the 1970s — it seemed that it would be impossible to improve on this outstanding record, already the best in the English game. But in the new decade, teams from Anfield were to record even more impressive achievments.

PLAYING THE GAME THE LIVERPOOL WAY

Is there a set pattern to Liverpool's play? Is there anything they do on the pitch that makes them different from other teams? They certainly do the simple things well – and then have the players who do the complicated things superbly. But above all, they are a unit that makes the most of the strengths of the individual footballer.

Liverpool's playing style was summed up in 1973 by Joe Mercer, former Manchester City manager, when he said: 'Liverpool are the most uncomplicated side in the world. They all drive forward when they've got the ball, and they all get behind it when they haven't.' Sixteen years later, at Wembley, during the 1989 FA Cup Final against Everton, Kenny Dalglish's team once again demonstrated this

simple, but superb, way of playing the game when, Ian Rush scored a goal that summed up the Liverpool style of attacking play.

The move began with a ball played out of the Liverpool penalty area to Steve Staunton on the right. Staunton ran with the ball before passing it short to Ray Houghton on his left. The Eire international then tried to run forward with the ball, realised his way was blocked, turned and played the ball back to Staunton, who had been following up. Staunton then pushed the ball to his left to Ronnie Whelan, racing unmarked into the centre circle. By now, Liverpool were getting their midfielders forward in numbers and so pushing Everton back into their own penalty area. Whelan immediately passed the ball to Steve McMahon on his left, who quickly played it to John Barnes, unmarked on the left wing. Barnes then released an early pass into the area, where all Ian Rush had to do was simply dip his head to steer the ball into the back of the net. Constant support leading to the final result of a great goal.

'Support the man and look for the ball' – the Shankly creed

Like so much else in the club, Bill Shankly's legacy lies at the very heart of this playing style. 'Support the man, look for the ball,' was a favourite motto. 'Never pass the ball to where there's one red shirt if there's two in another direction,' was another. The emphasis Shanks placed on a fluid approach and keeping possession led to great success. Managers visiting Anfield would sometimes complain there were more than 11 Liverpool players on the pitch — and one even counted the number of players as they left the field at the end of a game in which his team had been thoroughly roasted!

There is no doubt that Liverpool still play the system that has served them very well over the years. There is no real secret to it — it is simply that they support the man on the ball, and give him the right options. When they have possession, they give the opposition very few chances to get the ball back, and therefore play the game at their own pace. What is unusual is how they have been able to keep this system running so smoothly and with so few hiccups over the decades. The style remains the same, but the personnel alters.

Inculcating the good habits may take some time. Players have been bought from clubs, and then spent a considerable period in the reserves before they make it to the first team, all the time imbibing the Liverpool style. Liverpool were one of the first sides to use 5-a-side games as a staple of their practice routines — and

Ian Rush celebrates another great Liverpool moment with Peter Beardsley (left) and John Barnes. In the late 1980s, Rush became part of a three-man attack, whereas in the middle years of the decade he formed a partnership with Kenny Dalglish. It would be hard to say which was the better forward line.

in 5-a-side, possession is everything.

The actual playing formation may change — by a little or by a lot — when a new player arrives. Some players may simply slot into a role, but this is rare. Most new players change in detail the way that the side approaches a game, because their strengths may lie in slightly different areas to the man they have replaced. During the 1980s, Liverpool have drastically overhauled the three basic areas of a football team — the defence, the midfield and the strikers — not just once but sometimes two or three times, and they have come up with the right result each time.

The deadly partnership: Kenny Dalglish and Ian Rush

Take the strikers first. When Kenny Dalglish joined the club in 1977, after the club's first European Cup triumph, there were big question marks over how he would fit in. He was replacing the live-wire Kevin Keegan, and yet was obviously a very different kind of player. He had often been used in a midfield role, or playing behind the strikers, for both his former club, Celtic, and by Scotland. At Liverpool, however, the team seemed to flow even better with the new player than it had when Keegan was up front. Dalglish's sense of position, his strength at resisting challenges from behind and his speed on the turn had suddenly given the club a new set of strengths, strengths that were a corner-stone of the successes of the late 1970s.

For the early 1980s, the question the club had to ask itself was who to use as a partner for Dalglish — and then the question became how to replace him. In the 1979-80 season, Dalglish's most regular partner was David Johnson, formerly of Everton and Ipswich. Johnson fitted in as a target man who could release the players around him at the right moment. A regular substitute was another forward, David Fairclough, 'supersub'. Fairclough had the knack of coming on and using his pace to get past defenders to score goals, but never fully established a first-team place. In the 1980-81 season, Liverpool began experimenting with other forwards to partner Dalglish. This season was one of experiment in all areas of the team, and 23 players were used, in contrast to just 17 in the season before.

Among the new forwards who were given opportunities were winger Howard Gayle, who, in one of his first performances, gave a brilliant display against Bayern Munich in the European Cup semi-final. But the key face was that of Ian Rush, who had a quiet start: in his first seven games during the 1980-81 season, he failed to score at all. In the 1981-82 season, however, Rush's deadly finishing became one of the talking points of the game. He scored 30 goals in just 49 outings, and the next season again scored 30. His partnership with Dalglish was extremely productive — in that same 1982-83 season, Dalglish had also scored 20 goals. And this was in spite of the fact that, owing to

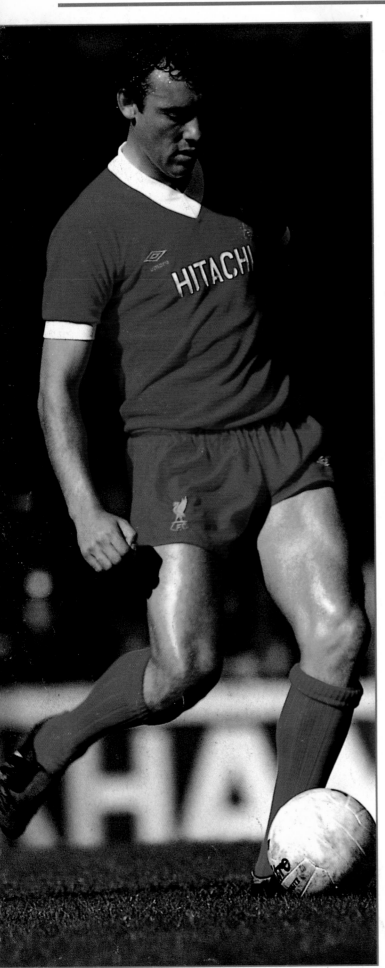

injuries, Dalglish often had to play in a deeper position, with his place up front taken by David Hodgson, who had been bought from Middlesbrough.

In Rush and Dalglish, Liverpool possessed perhaps the two most feared forwards in the Football League. Dalglish was the master craftsman at pulling his man out of position, and running the game from the front of the team, whereas Rush had that electric burst of speed into the box, often pursuing a short through ball played by his illustrious partner. He had the classic goalscorer's instinct of being there in space when the ball came to him in the penalty area. His talent, however, had its limits, and he was nothing like as effective when he went to Juventus for a season. He was glad to return to Anfield after one unhappy season in the Italian sun.

Buying cover and buying a successor to Kenny Dalglish

Apart from Hodgson who was bought as cover, Liverpool bought a traditional centre-forward — Michael Robinson — for the 1983-84 season, when Joe Fagan took over from Bob Paisley as manager. Robinson's bustling style did not seem quite in keeping with the elegant Liverpool game, but Fagan's judgment was vindicated in that season when, with Dalglish out with a depressed fracture of the cheekbone, Robinson proved a sound target man, who took the pressure of Rush.

The 1984-85 season that climaxed in the disaster at the Heysel stadium was one in which Liverpool won no trophies, and Kenny Dalglish was named manager of the club in succession to Fagan. Dalglish was now considering himself to be getting near the end of his playing career, and the replacement seemed to be Paul Walsh, a talented young forward bought from Luton in the 1983-84 season but who had not been given a run in the first team in the 1984-85 campaign. In the 1985-86 double-winning year, Dalglish often played himself as substitute, and came through as a major influence towards the end of the season. This season brought great success — but the following one did not. Walsh was not proving to be the ideal partner for Rush, and the Welsh goal king himself announced that he would leave at the end of the season.

While Dalglish had been able to buy John Aldridge, a player with an uncanny physical resemblance as well as a similar deadliness about his finishing, to replace Rush, he believed that the forward line that he and Rush had created needed to be completely altered. So in the summer of 1987, he went into the transfer market in a big way, and bought John Barnes and Peter

Ray Kennedy was converted from a ponderous striker to a midfield distributor, whose cultured passing opened up many a defence, especially for his midfield partner Terry McDermott.

Beardsley, paying Watford £900,000 for Barnes and Newcastle £1.9 million for the established England international Beardsley.

Aldridge, Barnes and Beardsley: the three-man attack

The combination of Aldridge, Barnes and Beardsley proved absolutely devastating. None of the players was a conventional 'target man' or had the strength that Dalglish had shown in this position, but they fitted in superbly. Barnes essentially played down the left, but often moved inside when heavily marked and sometimes played a floating role; the team would be looking for him just as once they had been looking for Dalglish. His job was not to get involved in a midfield battle, but to be ready to use his dribbling skills to set up goals. Beardsley was a mobile, terrifically skilful forward, whose speed and close control made him a threat wherever he received the ball. And Aldridge was ready to pounce when the ball came free in the area.

When Rush returned from Italy, this system hardly changed: Aldridge and Rush occasionally played together, but their styles were not complimentary, and, after some soul-searching, Dalglish decided to go for Rush as his first choice and sold Aldridge to Real Sociedad in 1989. So the club ended the decade with a forward line that operated in a very different way from the unit that had begun the 1980s.

Passing, running and tackling: the midfield blend

In midfield, the same progression was evident. The side that lifted the trophy in the 1979-80 season boasted one of the finest midfield combinations of all time — and all of them were encouraged to play to their strengths. Ray Kennedy was an excellent passer of the ball, and good at resisting challenges. Kennedy was no race horse; but he was not expected to be. Bob Paisley, who had converted him from a slowing striker to a midfield master in 1974, did not expect him to run all around the park. The running was done by Terry McDermott, who had enviable stamina, and a great eye for space. Then there was Jimmy Case, a predominantly right-sided player who had two great strengths. The first was his shot, one of the hardest in the First Division, and the second was his ferocious tackling. Case had a very good understanding with the elegant right-back Phil Neal in attack. The Kennedy-McDermott and Case-Neal combinations gave the team that entered the decade

On the receiving end of many of Ray Kennedy's passes, Terry McDermott could run all day, and was the engine of the team, always covering in defence and moving into dangerous positions up front.

great solidity in keeping possession of the ball — a vital part of the team's style of play.

Knitting all this together and pulling the strings was Graeme Souness — at this period the best all-round midfield player in the game. Souness would have been happy to go for a 50-50 ball with Case — or anyone else in the world for that matter. His uncompromising physical presence did not allow for any intimidation, — the captain of the Romanian team Dinamo Bucharest who tried to intimidate the Liverpool midfield ended up with a broken jaw. Souness was a great creator — typical Liverpool moves of this period always flowed through him.

This well-balanced midfield was being changed by Liverpool as early as the 1980-81 season, however. During that transitional period, players such as Sammy Lee, Ronnie Whelan and Kevin Sheedy were all given games. Lee rapidly established himself, partly because Case was suffering from a knee injury. Case left in August 1981, and became one of the very few players the club let go too early — his continued success for Southampton, even as the decade was ending, testified to his complete recovery from the injury that Liverpool

thought had shortened his career. Lee continued where Case had left off in his partnership with Phil Neal on the right, and his non-stop running became a key part of the side's balance.

Creating a new midfield with Lee, Whelan and Johnston

Whelan established himself the next season, scoring goals freely and replacing Ray Kennedy as a predominantly left-sided player. Then, in the 1982-83 season, Paisley's last as manager, Craig Johnston, who had been bought from Middlesbrough back in April 1981, established himself in the team. Both Ray Kennedy and Terry McDermott left Liverpool in 1982; three out of four of the midfield of the 1980 side had changed in two years. This new midfield had some

BELOW: Sammy Lee was a considerable force down the right, where his link with full-back Phil Neal was an important part of the Liverpool pattern. Lee's great gifts were his running and passing.

similar balances to the old one: there was a left-sided player in Whelan and a forceful right-sided player in Lee, for example. But Whelan covered more ground than Kennedy, and was stronger in the air defensively; he did not have Kennedy's magical weight of pass, but he soaked up more space. Johnston did not have McDermott's unselfish willingness to run all day — but he had greater dribbling skill, and was quicker over those vital five yards near the box.

Finding a hard man – Steve McMahon replaces Graeme Souness

This side won the League Championship and the League Cup in the 1982-83 season, but new manager Joe Fagan continued buying midfield talent, adding Ipswich's John Wark, who had an unmatched goal-scoring record for a midfield player, to the squad early in 1983. Wark's opportunity to show what he could do came in the next season, because Souness left Liverpool for Italian side Sampdoria at the beginning of the 1984-85 season. Kevin MacDonald from Leicester was brought in as well, but although there were some good performances and Wark scored 27 goals, there were no trophies that season, and new manager Kenny Dalglish faced the coming season with the spectre of Heysel hanging over the team.

The midfield was to change quite decidedly in this new season, when Liverpool bounced back to win the double. One new player who performed well was Jim Beglin, but the real change came in the presence of Dane Jan Molby, who had struggled when he had joined the club from Ajax the previous season, and Steve

...while Phil Neal was always comfortable on the ball and prepared to dribble past an opponent, provided that Lee was covering him. Neal played 630 times for the club and was Bob Paisley's first signing. He also collected 50 England caps.

McMahon, who was bought from Aston Villa.

Between them, McMahon and Molby made up for the loss of the skills of Graeme Souness and Ray Kennedy. McMahon was a tough tackler with a fierce shot, while Molby had the gift of seeing play and threading the ball into the right place. Molby also possessed Souness' gift of spotting an opening and going aggressively for goal. It was interesting, though, that Dalglish often used Molby as a sweeper.

Changes on the right as Sammy Lee and Phil Neal move on

McMahon's acquisition led to the gradual eclipse of Sammy Lee, (who left the club the following season) — a process that was mirrored in the eclipse of Phil Neal, Lee's ally on the right flank. So the great midfield that had entered the 1980s had been profoundly changed not once but twice by the middle of the decade, in a calculating manner that slotted players in at just the right time, and did not alter the basic balance of the team — but certainly gave it new options as some of the old ones closed.

In the 1986-87 season, the midfield underwent few changes, although Dalglish bought Nigel Spackman from Chelsea to use as a full-back or defensive midfielder, but the fact that full-back Steve Nicol was

frequently used in midfield, that Spackman had been bought and that players such as Jim Beglin alternated between full-back and midfield pointed to the way that Dalglish would organise his team during the late 1980s.

A new role for the forwards and a new role for the midfield

With the purchase of Barnes and Beardsley and their prolific combination with John Aldridge, the team had a rather different shape from that of the early 1980s, when an axis from Alan Hansen at the back through Graeme Souness in midfield to Dalglish up front had defined play. Now, while Hansen was still there at the back, the formation used in midfield or defence became more fluid, and the possession game had the object of releasing the ball skills of the men up front. By the end of the 1987-88 season, when Liverpool had played some of the best football in their illustrious history, the first-choice midfield was Ronnie Whelan on the left; the energetic Ray Houghton on the right wing (he was bought in October 1987 from Oxford); and Steve McMahon holding things together in the middle.

Whether the midfield that entered the 1990s is as good as the midfield that entered the 1980s is a moot point, and one that highlights the strengths of Liverpool in finding the right team blend. For although the present midfield has perhaps not the breadth of footballing talent — and certainly has no player to compare with Graeme Souness — its role is somewhat different. The skills of Barnes and Beardsley give the side a penetration that the two-man attack of Dalglish and his single partner — be it David Johnson, David Fairclough or even Ian Rush — did not have.

The long shadow of Alan Hansen, core of the defence

In defence, too, there has been a story of slotting in new players, and developing play. But there has been one bed-rock on which the team has relied — Alan Hansen. He joined Liverpool from Partick Thistle in 1977, but did not get an extended run in the first team for some time, being used as a deputy for Emlyn Hughes and Phil Thompson, the first-choice central defenders in the late 1970s. He performed in the European Cup Final of 1978, however, and then replaced Hughes as Phil Thompson's regular partner. Hansen's long career, and the way he plays, says everything about the way that Liverpool Football Club approach the game.

Graeme Souness was the greatest midfield player that Liverpool fielded during the 1980s. His subtle control, thunderous shooting and astute reading of the game were matched by an uncompromising hardness that often intimidated opponents.

Since the departure of stopper centre-half Larry Lloyd in 1974, the team had decided to play with more mobile, skilful players in the centre of defence, players able to turn quickly when defending, but also able to carry the ball forward and keep possession when required. There has always been, therefore, a question mark over the team's ability to withstand sustained aerial bombardment — as their defeat by Crystal Palace in the semi final of the 1989-90 FA Cup (when Palace's critical goals came from high balls floated into the penalty area) perhaps illustrated. What the team gains more than compensates, however. The Liverpool style of defence is quite simply not to let the opposition have the ball — while they are not in possession, they cannot attack.

Phil Neal and Alan Kennedy – contrasting style at full-back

In this style, Hansen has been a key part of the side. No player in the British Isles over the past decade has been better than him at bringing the ball out of defence, beating a man to open up space, always being available as a last resort to change the point of attack. Although not a scorer of goals (his record tally for any one season is just four goals), he can dominate play with bursts through the middle and shrewd passes. His paltry record of 26 Scottish caps says little for the selectors of the national side for whom he should have been a key player. Of the three-man axis that brought the club into the 1980s — Souness, Dalglish and Hansen — 'big Al' is the only one still there playing — suffering from knee trouble and one of the oldest members of the side. It is difficult to see how he can be replaced and it will be interesting to see how the club does it.

The defence that Hansen graced in the early years of the decade featured two full-backs of contrasting styles. Alan Kennedy on the left was a fast, burly, aggressive player with a knack of scoring important goals (including two — one in a penalty shoot out — that won European Cups) and a considerable physical presence that meant that Ray Kennedy's comparative slowness into the tackle was not a serious problem on the left. On the right was Phil Neal, Bob Paisley's first signing in 1974, and a wonderfully consistent player who played 630 times for the club. Neal had an excellent positional sense, and very good close control. As he aged, his lack of speed on the turn was often pointed out, but rarely exploited, because with Jimmy Case and then Sammy Lee playing with him, he had adequate cover and a good foil going forward. So on the flanks, this team knitted together well.

Steve McMahon brought strength in the tackle to the Liverpool midfield of the late 1980s, making it difficult for opponents to run at the central defence and providing a steely resilience to replace the defensive skills of Souness.

23

In the centre, the club's first concern was to replace Phil Thompson, who was spindly looking but very quick in the tackle. The team needed adequate cover at centre-back, because the departure of experienced players such as Tommy Smith and Emlyn Hughes in the late 1970s had reduced the options available. Young players such as Colin Irwin and Richard Money were tried, and Avi Cohen was bought from Tel Aviv. Irwin and Money performed very well in the 1980-81 season, and Irwin's more conventional approach looked as though it would be a good foil for Hansen's skill, but in August 1981 Paisley saw the player he wanted. He bought Mark Lawrenson from Brighton for £900,000.

The perfect central defence: Hansen and Lawrenson

Until Lawrenson suffered an injury that prematurely ended his career in the 1987-88 season, his partnership with Hansen was the best in the Football League, and maybe the best in Europe. Lawrenson would have qualified in most of these years as one of the best defensive players in the world: he was tall, ruthless and uncompromising in the tackle, very fast

Everton's Adrian Heath winces as Mark Lawrenson dives into the tackle. Lawrenson was perhaps the best defender in Europe during his Liverpool years. He had everything – pace, strength, power, ability in the air and a totally professional temperament. Many forwards believed they had got past him, only for the former Brighton player to turn rapidly and recover within a couple of yards.

and very quick on the turn. Add these qualities to the speed and elegance of Hansen and Liverpool had the best central defence in their history.

As cover for Hansen and Lawrenson, Joe Fagan bought Gary Gillespie from Coventry in 1983. Gillespie was again a skilful defender, able to fit the role of carrying the ball forward and retaining possession where necessary. At full-back, there were changes by the mid-1980s. Phil Neal was gradually replaced by Steve Nicol, who had come to the club in 1981 from Ayr United. Neal left in December 1985, following Alan Kennedy who had gone earlier that season. Jim Beglin took over the left-back spot, bringing greater ball skills to the position.

Both Nicol and Beglin (who unfortunately broke a leg in the 1986-87 season) were more than conventional

Bob Paisley pats 'Barney Rubble' (full back Alan Kennedy) affectionately after the 1983 Milk Cup Final that the club won against Manchester United with goals from Kennedy (who had a habit of scoring on the big occasion) and Ronnie Whelan. Back Row from left: Mark Lawrenson, David Fairclough, Alan Hansen, Ronnie Whelan, Ian Rush and Bruce Grobbelaar; front row from left: Craig Johnston, Kenny Dalglish, Phil Neal, Graeme Souness, Sammy Lee and Alan Kennedy.

Club choose its players? How does it treat them? And how do they get on with each other and with the men who run the club?

There are three ways of obtaining players for a leading club side — spotting them young and bringing them up through youth teams, buying ready-made stars, who have already shown what they can achieve at the level of the First Division or other top football, or buying talent that is just showing itself in a lower division and looks promising.

Liverpool are no exception to this rule. They have, however, differed from clubs such as Arsenal and Manchester United in that they have placed less emphasis on the products of their youth policy. Partly this has been through being constantly on top during the 1980s, and never having been able to 'blood' young players in something less than the most demanding of environments. For Liverpool are always the club to beat — every game they play brings players under close scrutiny and under great pressure. Not for young Liverpool players the opportunity to blend into the side in the Second Division (an opportunity Tommy Docherty's Manchester United players of the mid 1970s grasped) or to fit together as a mid-table outfit while the Merseyside giants battled it out for the honours, like George Graham's Arsenal side of the late 1980s.

The youth policy – not making promises you can't keep

There has also been some amount of deliberate policy, in that the club accepted that it would probably have to rely on bought players. Nevertheless, from Sammy Lee in the earlier years of the decade to Gary Ablett in the 1990 League-winning side, there has been a route to the top for local boys. Sammy Lee had been given trials at Everton when he was 14, but at the age of 16 he signed forms for Liverpool: 'I think Everton thought I would go back to them when I finished school, and Coventry came in too. But I was impressed with Liverpool because Tom Saunders [then Youth Liaison Officer] was so honest and straightforward with me. He told me, "It's all down to yourself." He wasn't making promises he couldn't keep.'

Lee's life as an apprentice was typical of that of other apprentices in the Football League. It began at nine o'clock in the morning, when he arrived at the ground. He undertook basic tasks, such as laying out the kit and making sure the baths were clean. He also had to clean the boots of a more senior player. But at 17 he became a full professional and his routine changed — arrival time at the ground was now ten o'clock for the regular training with the main squad. Lee described at the time how the whole Liverpool set contributed to his development as a player: 'I was under Roy Evans for a few years and he was certainly a big influence, but Bob Paisley, Joe Fagan, Ronnie Moran, Tom Saunders...they have all been equally helpful because at this club everybody speaks to everybody else and helps each other out. It's the good thing about Liverpool.'

Buying big, but making sure it's buying the right player

It is certainly true that players bought when their careers have already begun made up the vast majority of the Liverpool squad in the 1980s. But in the stakes of spending big, Liverpool have, in fact, been remarkably astute. From the signing of myself and Ron Yeats in the 1960s through to the snapping up of Kenny Dalglish in 1977 and the buying of John Barnes and Peter Beardsley in 1987, the club has never been afraid to spend money on players. But what they have got is the right players.

The purchase of Barnes and Beardsley is often used as an example of Liverpool being able to buy success. But it is interesting that no other club came in with a bid for Barnes when he was about to leave Watford. In retrospect — after a season in which the club played some of its best football ever — Barnes was seen as England's most talented footballer. But only after that season with Liverpool.

Buying top stars is not, then, the simple matter that it might appear to be; and, in fact, Liverpool have not used this method of acquiring players to anything like the same extent as other clubs. Where they have scored is in getting players, from the lower divisions or from less successful First Division clubs, who can fit into the Liverpool style.

Cash on the nose and a reasonable offer

The Liverpool style is not to try to get players on the cheap. The club believes in paying the right price, and they normally go in with a bid that they feel is reasonable. Not for them the policy of finding that a player is disaffected and so they might be able to pick him up for less than his market value. Nor do they haggle about terms of payment, trying to pay in instalments. They pay the fee there and then. And finally, for the player himself, the salary they offer often comes as a pleasant surprise. Alan Hansen, the player who performed throughout the decade and was uindoubtedly one of Bob Paisley's best buys, has described how his transfer from Partick Thistle took place with minimum fuss and maximum efficiency. Scot Symon, general manager of the Scots club, was, says Hansen, surprised and delighted by the manner in which Liverpool operated: 'There was a certain style about the way the club secretary Peter Robinson told him that the cheque had been made out and that they would give it to him to take home to Glasgow on the train that night. I can still remember going back north after all the signing formalities had taken place and Mr Symon kept pulling out the cheque for £100,000 and looking at it with awe. He seemed stunned because so many transfer deals are handled differently.'

Hansen was not only impressed with the general way that the club handled the deal; he also found that he himself was going to get three times the money he had been on at Partick. Then, after Hansen had been at the club for a year, and had played some first-team games, including the European Cup Final against Bruges, he was called into Peter Robinson's office and told that his salary had been doubled. The year after that, Hansen was informed that his bonus was to be increased — because he had begun his international career with Scotland and the club's policy was to give internationals extra money. His description of subsequent wage negotiations is of how simple they have been: 'I've gone in with a salary figure in mind, and I've usually found that they have had a figure very close to mine under consideration...I haven't had the slightest problem with contracts.'

Bruce Grobbelaar at his most athletic, stretching to a shot. Grobbelaar has been a Liverpool fixture since Ray Clemence's move to Spurs in 1981, and his eccentricities (both on and off the field) are now part of the character of the club.

John Aldridge, who joined the club in the late 1980s, confirms Hansen's impression. His departure from Oxford United was complicated, he feels, because Robert Maxwell, who owned Oxford, had newspaper interests that affected the way he looked at the game. When he met John Smith, Kenny Dalglish and Peter Robinson to discuss the transfer, he found he was in a different world, where the player had to feel happy about what he was doing. The Liverpool officials agreed to give him the four-year contract he asked for, and when the subject of money came up, Aldridge has described how: 'I just blinked and thought, "That's incredible. That's almost double what I was getting at Oxford. " '

'...whatever is done is all over by the time it is announced in the press'

Settling down as a player at Liverpool is, in essence, no different to settling down at any other club — if unmarried, the player may inhabit a hotel until he can sort himself out, and, if married, he may have to do some long-distance commuting before he gets a suitable house in the Liverpool area. The club will provide hotel accommodation and will do everything necessary to ease the player into his new life.

Players who join Liverpool are aware that they have become part of the elite of the Football League. There are rarely second thoughts about becoming part of the set up. Settling down with the other players is another matter. On one level, there are few problems — professional footballers are aware of each other and each other's skills, and recognise the contribution that a new individual can make.

Kevin MacDonald, who joined the club in 1984 as a midfield player explained how easily he had settled down:

'I was signed by Liverpool in November. I did hear that the club had been watching me for about six months before. I'd played against them a few times and had reasonably good performances.

'The players realise that they are involved in a big club. The coaching staff treat everyone just as another lad. The other parts of the staff are kept very low key. If the club makes any of its moves it does so very silently and efficiently — so that whatever is done is all over by the time it is announced in the press.

'When I first moved up there, the team were very good at helping me settle in'

'When I first moved up there, the rest of the team were very good at helping me settle in. When Liverpool buy players they select those who will really fit in with the team. It's different being at Anfield, though. Because whereas some players will be the real stars of the team they have come from, at Liverpool they learn straight

Grobbelaar rues the way that fortune sometimes goes against the Reds. One of his greatest assets is that he keeps the game of football in perspective, and will not let the odd mistake or piece of bad luck affect his confidence.

away that they will not be treated differently from anyone else.

'I spent about a month or six weeks in the reserves when I arrived at Liverpool, but the team were going through an indifferent spell so I got into the team reasonably quickly. Some players can spend about seven months or more in the reserves.'

There is another level of fitting into the Liverpool team that is more difficult, however. The players are renowned for a very dry sense of humour, and of not sweeping anything under the carpet. Any player has to be able to cope with this. When John Aldridge was involved in a fracas in a bar and was taken to court, the rest of the squad did not let the incident hang in embarrassed silences, as Aldridge described at the time: 'I'm happy to forget all about the nightmare, although the lads are doing their best to remind me. I have started to take terrible stick in the dressing room. "Don't hit me with that bottle!" is a favourite mickey-take.' And when Jan Molby served a three-month jail sentence for a motoring offence, the sign that he was back, according to Ray Houghton, was that he began receiving 'stick' from the rest of the squad 'which is a sure sign that the atmosphere between Jan and the club is back to what it was.'

But underlying all the banter is a certain amount of fear and anxiety. A professional footballer's life at the top is not very long at the best of times, and it can easily be curtailed by injury. New players coming into the squad can make things difficult for established members, and the competition for places is always keen. Under Kenny Dalglish, the team is not announced until the afternoon of the match day, and so there may well be some disappointed players who have been half hoping that they might be included.

The squad system: who gets left out of the side?

The squad system of 15-16 players is vital to maintain a championship challenge, and so, inevitably, not everyone can play. This can lead to a nagging insecurity and doubt. John Aldridge, who had had a wonderful season when Liverpool set up their new forward line with him, Peter Beardsley and John Barnes in the 1987-88 season, has recorded his feelings when he heard on the radio that Liverpool had bought Ian Rush back from Juventus: 'I just couldn't believe it. Rushie is a good friend but I have to admit that my first reaction was to be gutted. The thought that flashed through my mind was: is my position in the side at risk? Two days before the start of a new season, it was the last thing I needed...Football is an amazing career. You can feel on top of the world one minute and down the next...I had just built myself up for another season when another bombshell comes along.'

And midfielder Ray Houghton put down at the time the thoughts that ran through his mind: 'It means pressure on the rest of us, because, if John and Ian are in the side, Peter Beardsley will either have to drop out or push back into a deeper role and then the finger will be pointed at the midfield positions.'

Dealing with long-term injuries and long-term problems

That same season, Nigel Spackman left the club, because he could not command a regular first-team place. In his diary, Ray Houghton described the move: 'I feel sorry for Nigel because he loved it at Liverpool, but, after much soul-searching, he decided to go simply because he couldn't get in the first team. He has only started 11 games...at the age of of 28, any professional needs first-team football and I can understand him making the decision to go.'

The club itself makes a deliberate point of trying to minimise these problems that footballers face, realising that they are a major worry. Kevin MacDonald, who suffered a broken leg after starring in the side that won the 'double' in the 1985-86 season said: 'The best thing about being a Liverpool player is that you are playing with the best team in Europe, if not the world and you know that you will be seriously challenging for a number of trophies every year. The fans are splendid and the whole community is really geared to football. The worst thing is when you get injured, or are dropped when Liverpool are having a bad run. Because if they hit form then it's quite likely that you might not get back in the side for another eight months. But even those players who are on the side-lines are treated very well. You go on the foreign trips and you are really made to feel part of it all.

'The club is special. I still have friends there and I still like to see them as often as possible. From a personal point of view, they were excellent to me. I broke my leg while I was there and I couldn't play for over a year. They still included me on all the trips. Although the players are spread about around Liverpool — only a couple lived in the city when I was there — there were quite a few occasions when we would go out for drinks. And the wives of the players got on well, so groups of us would go out for meals. The club were good as well. Three or four times a year they would organise a club do for the players and their families. That all helps when you go out on the pitch, it's better if you respect the other players. You certainly have to rely on them.'

Training lasts for 90 minutes – just like a League match

All aspects of preparing the players for their work on the park are conducted in a unique Liverpool style. The training, for example, at the Melwood training ground, has a routine that hardly varies. When Craig Johnston arrived at the club from Middlesbrough, his first training session was on a bitterly cold day. He wore tracksuit trousers on his way to the training ground, and was warned by a team-mate that he shouldn't wear them for training. He looked around the coach, and saw that all the players were wearing shorts; coaches Roy Evans and Ronnie Moran were wearing shorts; and when the training actually began, manager Bob Paisley walked out wearing shorts — with the veins in his legs standing out blue in the freezing temperature. The Liverpool theory was that players should train as they would play — and playing on a Saturday afternoon would involve wearing shorts, not a tracksuit.

The training itself usually lasts for 90 minutes — the length of a League football match. And almost all the training takes the form of the 5-a-side games that were developed under Bill Shankly. Kevin MacDonald explained how the system works: 'The manager and Ronnie Moran and Roy Evans do most of the training.

John Aldridge, a Scouser who achieved a lifetime's ambition when he joined the club in 1987 as a replacement for Ian Rush. Like many Liverpool signings he was impressed by the professional and efficient way that Liverpool went about getting his signature on a contract.

But the emphasis is on playing football. There are lots of five-a-side games interspersed with sprinting. The players treat the games of 5-a-side very competitively. If you aren't trying hard then you get shouted at. But having said that, most things are done efficiently and quietly.' The routine is adhered to in almost all circumstances — there were changes in February 1989 after a bad run, and some three-a-side matches were introduced. But there is nothing in this training that contains the secret of Liverpool's success, nothing that cannot be reproduced elsewhere.

Pre-season training: getting ready for a long campaign

Where there is a difference between Liverpool and other clubs is in pre-season training. Kevin MacDonald again explained the system:

'There is a difference in the pre-season training. At Liverpool it definitely doesn't have the physical intensity that it does at other clubs. Liverpool don't get you to an absolute peak, because they know that there will be a high number of games ahead in the coming season. Basically, pre-season at Liverpool is aimed at getting the players at the level where they are ticking over. Some teams who concentrate on getting people really physically fit sometimes do this and then do well in the early part of the season, but then fade away badly.'

Tea and biscuits on a Friday, fish suppers on a Saturday

The Liverpool routines that the players have to fit into don't just stop at the training field. There are all sorts of seemingly irrelevant procedures that are part of the life of the club. Friday mornings, for example, as described by Ray Houghton: 'A typical Friday which began, as always, with tea and chocolate biscuits. They must be opened by the same people each week and the gaffer has first go and his packet must have two chocolate sides together like a sandwich. It is just part of the amazing Friday routine which you have to put down to superstition. Ronnie always opens the other two packets. If we play on a Sunday the biscuit routine is switched to Saturday. We split into pairs with one player getting the tea and his partner going for the biscuits...It sounds childish, but Liverpool couldn't possibly prepare for a game without this routine.'

Or there is the 'fish supper' that the players get on the coach back from away games. Or the Christmas Party where the players (no wives are invited) have to

Craig Johnston, skilful and fast, was compared by some to Kevin Keegan – perhaps because of his hair style. Johnston felt that it was difficult to command a regular place, although he had an excellent record over several seasons.

wear fancy dress. Or the Friday evening meal at the Moat House Hotel if the team are playing at home, when the team, and Dalglish, all sit at set places around a table — and a practical joke played on reserves is that they are encouraged to sit at Dalglish's place, to try to upset the Boss's obsession with maintaining the routine.

Within these routines, the players often find that they have a lot of time on their hands, as John Aldridge pointed out: '...we seem to have so many hours to kill when we are together as a squad. If you are not careful, boredom can take over and ruin your days. On Easter Sunday, after a quick loosener at 11 o'clock, we went away to a hotel to prepare for United. Peter, Nigel, Kevin MacDonald and I went for a walk around Haydock racecourse to kill some time and 'Spackers' saved the weekend by producing a computerised golf game that really caught the imagination of the lads. We wasted hours pitching our skills against each other and the rivalry became intense. It sounds silly, but games like that are very important when the hours stretch ahead of you in a hotel.'

Pulling up the drawbridge and shutting away the media world

The players who live this enclosed life, going through the club's routines, whiling away the hours in hotel rooms or on a coach, eternally worrying about injury or about being dropped from the most talented team squad in the land, must also be absolutely prepared to accept that just as the club is loyal to them when they are injured, so they must be loyal to the club. Leaks to the press are not the way Liverpool go about things — if the manager wishes to keep an injury secret, so as not to give opposing teams any advantage, then it is kept secret — as Peter Beardsley's leg injury was kept secret at the end of the 1989-1990 season. The staff at Liverpool — both playing and non-playing — are adamant that, when necessary, the club will always be prepared to pull up the drawbridge, to shut outsiders out.

So the pressures on players at Liverpool are quite intense. It is a tribute to the club how few individuals find these pressures too much — perhaps the secret lies in the routines, the tea and biscuits and fish suppers that keep life with the club at a mundane, never-changing level, whatever the highs and lows of the season.

The routines, however, are not intended to turn the players into Boy Scouts, or to take them back to their schooldays. Liverpool treats the players like the adults they are, and expects them to take responsibility for a great deal. Some players, for example, may be prone to be overweight — but neither Sammy Lee not Jan Molby were ever given specific orders to get their weight down to a certain level. It was just assumed that they would be responsible enough to make sure that they were not too heavy to compete effectively.

Some players, whatever their intentions, find it hard to settle at Anfield. Howard Gayle, a winger who had one brilliant game for the club against Bayern Munich in 1981, feels that his career with the club was harmed because he was black. The banter that all players subjected each other to had a racial bias in his case, and he refused to accept it. To the club, this refusal was seen as his having a chip on his shoulder — to Gayle, brought up in the Toxteth working-class area of Liverpool, the comments were unacceptable; to the Liverpool set-up, if he didn't want to fit in, it was his problem.

Interestingly enough, John Barnes seems to have found it easier to cope with the problems of being a black player in the city of Liverpool, perhaps because he came from a background of relative affluence, far from the deprivation of Toxteth. In fact, Barnes took the offensive, showing his new team-mates that he could mix it in the chat stakes as soon as he arrived. There is a story that he was sitting at the Melwood training ground with two of his team-mates, just after he had arrived. The tea-lady brought the other two a cup of tea each. Barnes looked up and asked, 'What's wrong? Am I black or something?'

Taking the criticism and making the performances

Even the most established players at the club have to accept that their position can never be absolutely secure. Craig Johnston felt that it took him a long time to get established, and he has explained how he did not understand why he was sometimes dropped. This is possibly because he was often used as a utility player, when he would probably have preferred a more clear-cut

Ronnie Whelan played for most of the decade. His left foot gave the team balance, and some of his other skills – such as his power in the air – added to the all-round strength of the side. Above all, he played at a consistently high level, and was able to take whatever responsibility the club wanted without giving less than his best.

position. Other players with the club — Steve Nicol or Jan Molby, for example — were able to assume a variety of positions without feeling that they were not accepted or that their skills were devalued.

The most settled players at the club have to be prepared to endure criticism. Even Alan Hansen was not immune to criticism from his managers. In his early days with the club, Bob Paisley commented: 'Alan's skill is there for all to see. The query is his defensive work.' And when Joe Fagan took over, he confessed that he was pleased that his fears about Hansen had not all been realised: 'He's been a bit of a revelation to me lately. The big difference is that he's become a bit harder, a bit more professional in his attitude, and his game's been all the better for it.'

There are many players in the Football League who are more skilful than the players who pull on the red shirts of Liverpool Football Club. But sheer ability is not enough to give a club the success that Liverpool had. To play for Liverpool, a player has to have skill that ranks with the best. But he also has to have a certain spirit, to work for his team, to drive them on when things get

David Fairclough – 'supersub' – never quite established himself except as a regular substitute, although he had several extended runs in the first team, and yet he scored important goals, and his speed always worried defences.

tough. You don't win Championships by giving up in the last 20 minutes when you're 0-2 down — however unpromising the situation may seem.

Bill Shankly used to say, 'Don't let them see that you're hurt!' Liverpool don't like to see players lying on the ground. They don't like shamming. If a player even puts his hands on his hips during a game, Ronnie Moran will be out of the dugout and screaming at him.

Every Liverpool player has to want to slot into the Anfield machine. And what is, perhaps, the secret of the club's success is that the players who go there almost all end up feeling a great affection for Liverpool FC. They enjoy going back to the boot room, and talking to their former colleagues. For as professionals, they realise that the professionalism of Liverpool is second to none, and they cannot fail to respect that.

TAKING A DECADE BY STORM

As the new decade began, the big question was, could Liverpool keep up the run of success they had enjoyed during the 1970s? Bob Paisley's men soon showed that they meant business, and that there was to be no stopping the Anfield machine.

Various trophy–winning combinations have flourished at Anfield since the club's foundation back in 1892. But in 1982, the side Liverpool produced during Bob Paisley's penultimate season as their manager, was certainly one of the finest.

There is little doubt that the team Paisley and his back room team put together to win their 13th League Championship in May 1982 had exceptional qualities. In that season of transition at Anfield, Liverpool had climbed from 12th place at the freezing turn of the year to leapfrog Bobby Robson's Ipswich to take the title.

The side that celebrated this particular Championship victory after beating Spurs 3-1 on 15 May 1982 has a familiar ring now — Grobbelaar, Neal, Lawrenson, Hansen, Alan Kennedy, Whelan, Thompson, Dalglish, Lee, Rush, Souness. The dynamic development was the partnership formed between Kenny Dalglish and newcomer Ian Rush. In later seasons, it would become the deadliest strike force in the League.

Phil Thompson was the last of the players that Bob Paisley inherited in 1974 to leave the club, in 1985, after 450 first-team appearances. In the early 1980s, he was an important link between old and new.

The arrival of Rush with 17 League goals in 32 League appearances, and Ronnie Whelan, who scored 10 League goals in 32 appearances, strengthened a Liverpool team that earlier had been struggling to re-create the charisma which had marked their play in the 1970s, when Kevin Keegan and John Toshack had led the way in striking partnerships.

Rush's goalscoring and Dalglish's all-round sharpness — linked to fellow Scot and captain Graeme Souness's hard tackling and quick perception — were major factors in the making of a great side. But as a relieved Paisley said afterwards, sipping a brandy in the secret confines of the club boot room: 'You wouldn't have dreamed that we would have put that many results behind us since the New Year. At the end of the day, the 1982 Championship was the most difficult to win — but we did — and I'm very proud.'

The secret of success? Three Scots and one Welshman

Mark Lawrenson, looking back on those years of celebration which marked the start of the 1980s, believes that four players in the team were chiefly responsible for bringing greatness to Anfield. 'Three were Scots, and one was a Welshman,' Lawrenson says, modestly, not naming his Irish self. His own contribution at centre-back was by no means meagre. 'Alan Hansen made very few mistakes, and was inspirational to the team at the back, which, by the way, he still is. A great club man. Graeme Souness was another Scottish backbone, a wonderful leader, while Kenny Dalglish had that perfect understanding with Ian Rush. It was an exciting team to play in. We certainly did Bob Paisley proud before he stepped down in 1983.'

Dalglish had said on his arrival at Anfield from Glasgow Celtic that he joined Liverpool 'to become a better player. And also to win as many honours as possible, particularly in Europe.' This he certainly did, winning European Cup Winners medals in 1978, 1981 and 1984. Between 1982 and 1984, Liverpool's future manager was in the side that won three consecutive League Championships, a hat-trick of victories earned by only Arsenal and Huddersfield before them. And during this period, Liverpool monopolised the Milk Cup, winning it four times in succession. By 1984, with Joe Fagan having succeeded Paisley as manager, Britain's leading club had notched up their fourth European Cup victory in beating A.S. Roma in Rome, an achievement bettered only by Real Madrid in the 1950s. In such circumstances, why quibble about this Liverpool squad being the finest of them all?

Liverpool's tremendous form for much of the first half of the 1980s had been, in part, inspired by the rise of rivals — and a bogey team — in the form of Brian Clough's Nottingham Forest. Brian Clough and his assistant, Peter Taylor, had brought Forest out of the Second Division in 1977 — the year Liverpool won their first

European Cup — and turned them into such an electrifying combination that a year later, Forest won the League Championship seven points clear of Liverpool.

An early rivalry with Clough's Nottingham Forest

And, as if this act of East Midlands audacity wasn't enough to needle the men of Anfield, Brian Clough's team went on to win the European Cup final two years in a row, including, in the second victory in 1980, beating Hamburg, whose star attacker that night was a disappointed Kevin Keegan. Forest also won the League twice during this period. And just to rub salt into Liverpool's smarting wounds, Forest knocked Bob Paisley's side out of the European Cup in an early round in 1978. Forest's smothering, defensive tactics in the games between the two clubs did not endear them to Liverpool, and Bob Paisley was not gracious in defeat — a sure sign that he was worried.

Forest, however, began to decline after their second European Cup victory — 'We were never quite the same after that victory,' Trevor Francis recalls. The £1 million forward soon departed to Manchester City, and was a witness as Liverpool began to turn the thumbscrews year after year in the First Division for the remaining seasons of the decade.

On top at the beginning of the season and on top at the end

At the end of the 1978-79 season, an ecstatic Anfield crowd had hailed the winning of Liverpool's 11th Championship after defeating Aston Villa 3-0 with goals from Alan Kennedy, Kenny Dalglish and Terry McDermott. A new club record of 30 wins was established, along with a new defensive record of only 16 League goals conceded. Liverpool had been unbeaten at home in the League programme for the seventh time, and had lost only four games away. Four goals conceded at Anfield was the lowest in the club's history, and Ray Clemence kept 28 clean sheets, another record. Fifteen players were used during the 1978-79 season, four of them regulars — even though Liverpool had been dumped out of the European Cup by Forest, there would always be a special feeling of affection at Anfield for this particular Liverpool squad: Clemence, Neal, Alan Kennedy, Thompson, R Kennedy, Hughes, Dalglish, Case, Heighway, McDermott, Souness, Johnson, Hansen and Fairclough.

This firm had taken Liverpool to the top of the First Division in the second Saturday of the season and kept it there for the rest of the campaign. The system which had made Liverpool so devastatingly successful in post-war football was strong enough to launch the club into another string of brilliant achievements as a new decade came in.

Liverpool started the 1979-80 season as ruthlessly as they had finished the previous one. On 11 August at Wembley, they strolled to victory against the FA Cup holders Arsenal — it was a superbly organised team performance, and gave thorough warning of their intentions for the approaching campaign. Perhaps FA Charity Shield matches are not always the best yardstick to judge from, because players are still not up to peak fitness and fans are still relaxing in sunny climes, but Liverpool on this occasion were in exceptional form.

Goals by Terry McDermott (twice) and Kenny Dalglish left no doubt as to which team would set the League title pace. It was to be another standard setting season for Paisley's team — although winning the League Championship would not be the one-horse race of the season before. And there were disappointments in the three available cup competitions — defeats by Dynamo Tblisi, the Soviet Union champions, in the European Cup; in the FA Cup by Arsenal, after three exciting semi-final replays; and another ousting by their old bogey team, Nottingham Forest, in a two-leg League Cup tie semi-final. These Cup defeats alerted Paisley's management team that their team, although functioning smoothly in the title chase, still had weaknesses.

Liverpool's 'bread and butter', the League Championship

In the League — which Bill Shankly once described as Liverpool's 'bread and butter' — the old Anfield steam roller moved on relentlessly. Liverpool were again unbeaten at home, conceding only eight League goals. The Championship was finally won when Aston Villa were the visitors. It took only three minutes for Liverpool to go ahead. Sammy Lee picked up a ball on the right wing and put over a cheeky cross. In came Dalglish, all fire and brimstone, only to be thwarted by goalkeeper Jimmy Rimmer. Unfortunately for Aston Villa, the ball ran to McDermott, who returned the ball with an accurate chip across the six-yard box for Johnson to stick the ball into an empty net. Vintage Liverpool — and the crowd loved it.

The Kop were still rejoicing when Aston Villa had the impertinence to equalise — and it was an own goal by the Israeli international, Avi Cohen, a popular squad member in his day, that was responsible. Dead in front of the Kop, Cohen embarrassed himself by slicing the ball over Ray Clemence's head into the net. Liverpool came out in the second half with that well known determination in their eyes. With the Kop roaring them on, it took just five minutes for the Champions-elect to take the lead again. That bundle of mercurial power, Sammy Lee, one of the most loved of all Anfielders, took a

Jimmy Case, tough midfielder with a cannonball shot, and one of the few players that Liverpool let go too early – as Case reminded his former club with many good games for Brighton and, later, Southampton.

throw-in level with the 18-yard box. He found Johnson, who cleverly played the ball into the area to Dalglish. A snake-like twisting turn by the Scot was followed by an accurate cross into the Villa box for Cohen, who made up for his earlier misdemeanour by sweeping the ball into the net.

European Cup whitewash in the Soviet Union

Later, David Johnson got his second goal of the afternoon, after a precise move between Souness and Lee, when he rifled in a a marvellous 25-yard shot that hummed into the roof of Rimmer's net. Liverpool, now in total command, added a fourth through an own goal by Blake.

Winning the League by two points from Manchester United was compensation for the three Cup disappointments, especially the major one against Dynamo Tblisi. Having established a 2-1 lead at Anfield, Paisley and his boot room team were unhappy witnesses of a 3-0 whitewash defeat in the Soviet Union. The FA semi-final marathon dismissal by Arsenal also hurt, although Arsenal would go down themselves 1-0 through a Trevor Brooking header for West Ham at Wembley. And as for the Nottingham Forest victory in the League Cup, Clough's team would be found out themselves at Wembley — Andy Gray scoring the only goal of the game for Wolves.

A curious season thus passed into history — but Paisley had no intention of sitting back on his laurels. A new striker would be welcomed into Liverpool's office to sign transfer forms from Chester for £350,000. He was Ian Rush.

1980-81 starts badly – problems with scoring goals

Although Liverpool won another FA Charity Shield against West Ham, they started the 1980-81 League season uncommonly poorly, worrying their manager by winning only three out of their first seven League games. This would have constituted a reasonable start for some teams, but in Anfield terms, it was very poor. Their true form came in spasms, but even a few good patches only brought them a highly disappointing fifth place in the League, behind Ron Saunders's emerging Aston Villa — who a year later would win the European Cup. What was also bad from Paisley's point of view was a lack of consistent goalscoring in the League: Terry McDermott was the only team member to finish with double figures. Kenny Dalglish, a persistent double figures man, managed only eight goals. But there were major consolations elsewhere — and how.

A very significant debut took place in December when Paisley brought Ian Rush into the side against Ipswich at Portman Road instead of Steve Heighway. This was the season that Bobby Robson's Suffolk side won the UEFA Cup — so Paisley's decision was a risky one. Few of the East Anglian element in the 32,000 crowd would have realised that a new Anfield star was about to be born, although it was evident that the young Welsh striker, driven on by Graeme Souness's enthusiasm, was on the brink of a promising future.

'I went out knowing that we wouldn't lose. That's the Souness psychology'

Rush still vividly remembers the afternoon — in his autobiography he recalled, and still recalls, eyes twinkling, how: 'Graeme went round every player at half time, fist clenched, geeing us up, telling us the game was ours for the taking. He had me feeling like a Superman. Then Joe Fagan and Ronnie Moran joined in, they kept pumping the adrenalin into us, saying "You can win this, you know you can. Show 'em what you are all about." Strange — I can't really explain the feeling to this day. But for the only time in my career I went out knowing that we wouldn't lose. That's the Souness psychology for you.'

Liverpool drew 1-1 that pre-Christmas afternoon with a goal scored by substitute Jimmy Case, who had replaced the injured David Johnson. By the New Year, they were on course to reach the Finals of the Milk Cup and European Cup with young Rush waiting starry-eyed in the wings having returned to the Central League side to bide his time. There was plenty of reserve talent in those days on Liverpool's books — Steve Ogrizovic, Colin Irwin, Jimmy Case, Howard Gayle among them, but Paisley was not easily led into making changes.

A League Cup Final decided by a questionable goal

Liverpool's opponents in the League Cup Final at Wembley that season were West Ham, the FA Cup holders. Rush and his reserve team buddies watched from the stands as the Final entered extra time. A goalless draw looked inevitable. Then Liverpool took a sudden lead through Alan Kennedy that had much to do with a much criticised decision by the Welsh referee, Clive Thomas, who ruled the goal a good one despite Sammy Lee lying prone on the grass in a blatantly offside position. Thomas had upset teams in the past, notably Ipswich and Brazil, and here he was again in the limelight. It looked odds on now that the League Cup would be in Anfield's hands by early evening. But in the last minute, West Ham were awarded a penalty. Ray Stewart coolly beat Clemence and the game ended in a draw.

Because of fixture congestion, the replay at Villa Park was played more than two weeks after the Wembley final. In the first game, another injury to David Johnson had meant a place for Steve Heighway, but a subsequent injury to the Irishman meant a place in the replay

for Rush, who could hardly believe his good fortune. Dalglish and the unfortunate Johnson had done wonders in raising Rush's morale, although he still felt shy among so many stars.

West Ham made a good start, and in the ninth minute Paul Goddard gave the East End side an early lead. It was a lead West Ham held until the 25th minute, when Dalglish equalised with a splendid goal. Alan Hansen eventually scored the winner — and the team that took the trophy at Villa Park had begun to look one ready to triumph in the future: Clemence, Neal, Alan Kennedy, Thompson, Ray Kennedy, Hansen, Dalglish, Lee, Rush, McDermott, Case. Liverpool, who had shunned the League Cup in it's pioneer days, regarding it as an extra burden, were now the proud winners of it for the first time.

The 1981 European Cup – bad game but good result

It says much for Liverpool's high degree of professionalism and intrepid spirit that they were able to return to the fray a few days after beating West Ham and take on the formidable West German champions, Bayern Munich, in the first leg of the European Cup semi-final at Anfield. They owed much again to the inspirational leadership of Graeme Souness whose verbal determination dominated the dressing room, pepping up the younger players.

Souness was now at the height of his senior playing career but he doubted whether Liverpool would overcome Bayern, even after a keenly contested 0-0 draw at Anfield. Rush, European inexperience allowing, did extremely well — and earned the praise of Brian Clough on television. In the second leg in Munich, Bayern felt arrogantly confident about reaching Paris — but a stunning goal from Ray Kennedy settled the match in Liverpool's favour and it was Liverpool who would fly to France.

A disappointing Final? — it was according to the media experts. Rush, who had gone into a Welsh sulk comparable to a Black Mountain mist on learning that he had not been selected even to sit on the substitute's bench, remembers the Final as being a 'containing battle which was won for us by a super goal by Alan Kennedy.' The first half was a niggly affair, although Ray Clemence did well to cut out one unpleasant in-swinger from the late Laurie Cunningham. Predictably, Johnson had his shirt torn by the sneaky Comancho who was keenly following Real's policy of man-to-man marking.

An unmemorable second half looked likely to stray into extra time as both teams struggled to live up to the

Michael Robinson attempts to round Gary Bailey during the 1983 Charity Shield match. Robinson was Joe Fagan's first signing (from Brighton for £200,000) and his bustling style proved a useful foil to Kenny Dalglish and Ian Rush.

form which had brought them to the Final. Then, in the 80th minute, Liverpool struck. They earned a throw-in deep inside the Real half. Ray Kennedy brushed aside Sammy Lee to take the throw, and found his namesake Alan who strode past two weak challenges and drove an unstoppable shot past goalkeeper Agustin. This was not a tremendous performance by Liverpool — but they earned the applause of the Parisian crowd afterwards. As captain Phil Thompson said after holding the coveted trophy aloft: 'We have joined the immortals.' Certainly it was another night of celebration for Paisley who was rapidly becoming the most successful manager ever to hold down a job in Britain, surpassing even the feats of Jock Stein at Celtic. The 1981 European Cup win was the third European Cup success in seven years as manager. And now the only man along with Phil Neal to play in all three of them would vacate his goalkeeping post in front of the Kop and move on to Spurs before the start of the 1981-82 season.

The departure of Ray Clemence and the arrival of the 'clown'

When Ray Clemence left Anfield in August 1981, he left behind 13 years of outstanding memories as Liverpool's regular first-team goalkeeper. The man in the green jersey from Scunthorpe had also won five League Championship medals, one FA Cup winners medal and played 656 times for his club. This was only one game less than Emlyn Hughes, who was second only to Ian Callaghan in overall appearances made for the club.

Clemence's marvellous positional sense and electric reflexes could always be depended on, not only by Liverpool, but by England. Much of Liverpool's successes in the 1970s had much to do with Clemence's agility. But now there was a time for change at Anfield, and the goalkeeper designated to replace Clemence would rapidly earn the dubious nickname 'clown'.

When Liverpool lined up for the first match of the 1981-82 season against Wolves, there were two new faces in the team. Centre-back Mark Lawrenson had been signed from Brighton to partner Hansen, and in goal was Bruce Grobbelaar, who would rapidly become not only one of the most colourful, but also one of the outstanding 'keepers in the world. Grobbelaar had been brought up in Rhodesia and done two years National Service there. He had played for the Vancouver Whitecaps in the North American Soccer League before being sent to Crewe Alexandra, for whom he played 24 League games.

Rush was not included in the Liverpool side for the Wolves match. Indeed, his lack of goals, even in the

David Johnson was unusual in that his career included successful spells at both Liverpool and Everton. He was very fast, and invaluable to his team-mates as he would always chase a pass, not just give up if it was less than perfect.

Central League, created doubt about his future. Rush was convinced he would never play for the first team again, calling himself 'a simmering kettle of discontent'. Paisley, however, remained calm, advising the young striker to go for goal, instead of laying the ball off all the time. Paisley was more concerned with the early performances of his team — a slow start to the first half of the season earned only six victories out of 16 by Boxing Day — deplorable by Liverpool standards. But then came that wonderful turn around to their fortunes described earlier in this chapter — and the ultimate winning of the title. Liverpool lost only two League games out of the last 25.

Rush, who had played seven League matches in the previous season and not scored, was recalled to the side and rapidly made his mark, scoring 17 League goals in 32 appearances including a hat-trick against Notts County at Anfield on Good Friday. Another to make his mark was the Australian Craig Johnston, who scored six goals in 18 appearances that season after joining the club from Middlesbrough.

New boy Ronnie Whelan clinches the 1982 Milk Cup...

There were mixed fortunes in the major Cup competitions, however. Liverpool were eliminated from the third round of the European Cup by the stylish Bulgarian side, CSKA Sofia, and from the FA Cup through a sensational victory 2-0 by Second Division Chelsea, who were in disarray at the time and near bankrupt. But Chelsea fought like tigers for their new manager John Neal and fully deserved victory. Liverpool later retained the League Cup, beating Spurs at Wembley after conceding a first goal scored by Steve Archibald. Spurs looked as if they would win until a memorable goal scored three minutes from time by new boy Ronnie Whelan. Liverpool then took charge and another goal from Whelan and a rejoicing, rejuvenated Rush gave Liverpool what had now become the Milk Cup. Overall, another splendid season at Anfield ended with the news that Bob Paisley would step down at the end of the next one. The task of replacing him would be a difficult one. The rotund, retiring Paisley, known for his love of racehorses and stables, had been little less than majestic as the leader of a great football team.

The Liverpool squad would have liked nothing better than to complete a grand slam for their retiring manager, Bob Paisley, in his last season in charge. Although Liverpool finished 11 points clear of second place Watford to clinch the League Championship, and continued their Milk Cup winning streak by beating Manchester United 2-1 after extra time, there were again disappointments. The most bitter came in the European Cup in March against the Polish side Widzew Lodz, who took advantage of a crass error by Bruce Grobbelaar in the first leg at Anfield to knock out their fancied English opponents. The FA Cup also brought a

shock, in the shape of a 2-1 fifth round home defeat by relegation threatened Brighton and Hove Albion. Liverpool were odds-on favourites to win that Sunday afternoon in front of a 44,868 crowd — but Jimmy Case, playing enthusiastically in Brighton colours against his old club, had other ideas and helped the Seagulls to a memorable win.

...and some old boys put Liverpool out of the FA Cup

Brighton took full advantage in restoring some pride to their sagging fortunes by reaching the Final before losing to Manchester United in a replay. Their manager was another old Anfield favourite — Jimmy Melia, who was warmly congratulated by Paisley, Joe Fagan and Ronnie Moran afterwards.

Grobbelaar's errors against the Poles did not endear him to the Kop. 'Jungle Man', as Bruce was nicknamed by his team-mates, had not been universally popular among Anfield supporters, who still regarded Ray Clemence as the best of them all. Grobbelaar's penchant for racing out of his penalty area to clear the ball, and little bursts of eccentricity when he clowned with the ball in front of impatient opponents, sent shivers down the spine. And the Liverpool players were plainly furious when his errors led to their elimination in that season's European Cup. It took Souness to calm down the rest of the side: 'Bruce admits his mistakes,' the Edinburgh-born Scot said, 'But he has kept us in so many games recently that he is entitled to the odd error. He'll be back.' How right Souness was — Bruce Grobbelaar became a firm favourite at Anfield subsequently — and was still in charge of the Liverpool net at the end of the 1980s.

Rush enters the history books with a Merseyside derby hat-trick

A memorable match took place at Goodison Park in early November, which was screened live on television. Liverpool's stunning performance against their neighbours produced world-class performances from Dalglish, Souness, Hansen and Rush that captivated a watching nation. It turned out to be a great day for Rush and a bad one for Neville Southall in Everton's goal. After Rush, twice, and Lawrenson had put Liverpool three up, Rush made his own special piece of history. As usual Dalglish was involved, playing a brilliant through ball to Rush who scampered away like a greyhound, hitting the post with his first shot, and then putting the ball away to register his third. It was the first

FOLLOWING PAGE: Ronnie Whelan celebrates a goal in the defeat of Barnsley in the FA Cup in March 1985. Behind Whelan is Rush, who got a hat-trick in the game, and to his left is John Wark.

Merseyside derby hat-trick since 1935, when Fred Howe had scored four for Liverpool at Anfield. Rush, after prompting from Sammy Lee, scored another solo goal to make the score line 5-0 — the biggest away win in a Merseyside derby since 1914. Between this game and 4 April, Liverpool lost only one League game — which ensured that they would take the title in a run that included many displays of style, confidence and skill.

Their Milk Cup victory was won in extra time against Manchester United with a sweetly curving shot from Ronnie Whelan — his third goal in two successive Finals. At the end, captain Graeme Souness ushered Bob Paisley to lead the team up the steps at Wembley to collect the Milk Cup. It was a memorable gesture by Souness and marked the first time a manager had led his team up the steps to the Royal Box. Paisley received a deserved ovation from the 100,000 crowd, beamed

Phil Neal and Alan Kennedy savour a great moment – Liverpool have just won the 1984 European Cup, and Kennedy himself scored the decisive goal in the penalty shoot out.

modestly and trudged down to the pitch again. His job at Anfield was about to end. For the Anfield Board there was the enormous job of replacing Paisley, who had won the Manager of the Year award a record six times. When he took over in 1974 he had said: 'I'll let the team do the talking for me.' He had indeed done so to great effect.

Joe Fagan begins by piling up the trophies

Paisley's successor, Joe Fagan, was another product of the boot room, and he had the best debut possible, for in the 1983-84 season Liverpool amassed the finest array of silverware in the club's history. Apart from the FA Cup which ended as it had before against Brighton and Hove Albion at the Goldstone ground, Liverpool went on to win the League Championship, the Milk Cup and the European Cup. Not a bad start for Joe Fagan who naturally enough succeeded Paisley as Manager of the Year.

When Liverpool clinched their 15th League Championship after a goalless draw at Notts County, Bruce Grobbelaar could congratulate himself on having kept 20 clean sheets in 42 League matches. And by winning the Championship on three successive occasions, Liverpool had equalled the record of Huddersfield and Arsenal.

Then there was the Milk Cup victory which followed a momentous Merseyside derby at Wembley — a 0-0 draw after extra time which was played in the very best of spirit. The replay at Villa Park was won by Liverpool in the 21st minute with a thunderous goal from Souness in his last year at the club.

The clown to the rescue for a fourth European Cup

With a fanatical Roma crowd yelling their heroes on that hot evening of 29 May 1984, Liverpool could not have expected any favours from their hosts, in the battle to win the European Cup Final. But a goal by Phil Neal after 13 minutes did wonders for team morale. Liverpool looked set to record yet another famous victory until a lovely centre from the Italian World Cup hero, Conti, in the 43rd minute found Pruzzo who headed it joyfully into the far corner. Despite the flair of Brazil's Falcao, the feverish running of Conti and the bravado of Cerezo, Liverpool hung on to force extra time. The match remained deadlocked and for the first time in the 28 year history of the European Cup, the destiny of the trophy would be decided by penalties.

The Liverpool players selected to take the kicks were Souness, Neal, Nicol, Rush and Alan Kennedy. Alan

Another triumph of 1984 was in the Milk Cup. Here, Bruce Grobbelaar gathers the ball safely, flanked by the best central defensive partnership in Europe – Alan Hansen and Mark Lawrenson.

Kennedy would have taken the first, but Nicol begged to be given the chance — and promptly missed. Then Roma's captain Di Bartolomei calmly stroked his penalty in: 1-0 to Roma. Neal calmly put Liverpool level, and then it was Bruno Conti's turn. Conti, however, was put out of his stride by Grobbelaar's clowning on his goal-line. He began wobbling his legs in theatrical fashion and swivelling his hips like a chorus girl. All too much for Conti — he shot high over the bar. Both Souness and Righetti netted to make the score 2-2. The Italians had complained to the referee about Grobbelaar's antics, but the goalkeeper had kept to the rules by keeping his feet firmly planted on the ground.

Rush then put his effort snuggly in Tancredi's corner — to put Liverpool in front again. Graziani stepped up to take his kick. The Italian crossed himself, while Grobbelaar let his head roll on his shoulders like a drunken sailor and swayed around on his rubber knees. Graziani ran up, struck the ball hard against the top of the crossbar and it went over.

It was now down to Alan Kennedy. If he converted his kick, the European Cup was Liverpool's. The big full back's shot was a masterpiece of calm under explosive pressure — Fagan's team had won another splendid victory. The Roman party went on until dawn. And genuine feelings of a job well done were expressed by a delighted Dalglish: 'Everyone at Anfield is good at their job,' he said. The 1983-84 season was certainly proof of that.

MANAGERS

Liverpool have had three managers during the 1980s: Bob Paisley, Joe Fagan and Kenny Dalglish have all presided over teams that reached the peaks. They were all very different personalities, but how different were they in the way they approached the job? And what were their relationships with the players like?

ven the best of managers have to call it a day some time. On the morning of 12 July 1974, the legendary Bill Shankly casually announced that he had decided the time had come to stand down as Liverpool manager: he was retiring. Nobody believed him. Was this another famous Shankly joke? How could a man with football in his veins even consider retirement? But it was true. He had had

enough and had made his decision as he walked around Wembley back in May taking his salute from the famous Koppites. He felt that he had achieved all he could and that the time had come to stand aside and let someone else take up the reins.

For days, the city of Liverpool was shell-shocked. Nobody could possibly succeed Shanks. The press, of course, was full of speculation. The name of Crystal Palace manager Malcolm Allison was mentioned, as were one or two others, but as far as the Board were concerned there was only one possible choice: Shankly's number two and loyal assistant over the years, Bob Paisley. Although reluctant to step into Shankly's shoes, Paisley accepted the honour with customary loyalty and determination. He was not one for the limelight but took up his appointment determined to make it work.

Bob Paisley – a Liverpool man since 1939

Bob Paisley was born on 23 January 1919, in the small northeast village of Hetton-le-Hole. He began his footballing days with the famed local amateur team Bishop Auckland, and in 1939 he won an FA Amateur Cup-winners' medal, a success that caught the eye of Liverpool and brought him to Anfield. But before he could don his boots and pull on a red shirt, the Second World War broke out. Although he made a few appearances for Liverpool during the early 1940s, he was away serving in the Army for most of the War. He returned to make his League debut on 7 September 1946 when the Reds thrashed Chelsea 7-4 at Anfield. He made 33 appearances that season as Liverpool swept to the League Championship.

Over the next nine seasons, the robust little half-back would go on to make 278 appearances for the club and notch up 13 goals, his most important coming when he played as a replacement for the injured Laurie Hughes in the 1950 FA Cup semi-final against Everton at Maine Road. His first-half lob set the Reds on the way to Wembley, but when the team was selected for the Final, Laurie had recovered and there was no place for Bob. So he could only watch his team from the sidelines. It was to be a valuable lesson for him later in his career, when he had to drop players from his own team. He at least could understand their feelings. Characteristically Paisley carried on. He won his place back and played on until the end of the 1953-54 season. That season, Liverpool finished bottom of the First Division and Paisley, by then 35 years old, decided it was time to retire. The then Liverpool manager, Don Welsh, realising Paisley's experience and knowledge, offered him a job on the back room staff. Paisley eagerly accepted and

Bob Paisley is the most successful manager that the British game has ever known, with his three European Cups alone taking him clear of any rivals.

when Shankly arrived in 1959, the former Liverpool half-back found himself working alongside the legendary Scot.

'To be replacing Bill Shankly, everybody said he was on a hiding to nothing'

Bob Paisley found some difficulty in emerging from the lengthy shadow cast by the legend of Shankly. Kevin Keegan, Liverpool's star forward of the time, explained how he saw some of the problems involved with the transition of power: 'Shanks was out of order in not showing more tact during the early part of Bob's tenure as manager. Bob had just taken on the hardest job in football. To be replacing Bill Shankly, everybody said he was on a hiding to nothing, that he was no more than a sparring partner for a couple of rounds until the club found someone else. Some of the players thought that as well, and we wanted to help Bob in every way we could.

'When we went to Melwood training ground, Shanks would be there, quite rightly using the facilities. But would it not have been better if he had used them in the afternoons, when Bob and the team were not there? The players would come into training and say, "Good morning, Boss," to Shanks and then greet Bob Paisley with "Good morning, Bob." Poor Bob must have wondered what was happening. It was an embarrassing situation. It could be argued that the facilities should have been open to Shanks, because he had built them. They were the fruits of his hard work, his ideas and his success. I just believe he should have used more discretion.

'I never wanted this job in the first place'

'I will never forget Bob's first team meeting. He leant with his back against the wall of the dressing-room at Melwood, which seemed somewhat symbolic. I could not help feeling sorry for him because he looked to be in an impossible position. "I never wanted this job in the first place," he told us. He might have pretended he wanted to be manager, but that was not Bob's style. When the real Bob came to light we discovered that he was not the hard man we had imagined him to be. He was no soft touch, but was instead a shy, modest man who always wanted to give credit to others. Once we got to know Bob our relationship with him was excellent and his confidence grew.'

Success for Paisley as the new Liverpool manager was not immediately forthcoming, and failure that first season led to a number of pundits suggesting that he was no adequate successor to Shankly. But within the year, he was to prove them wrong as his team carried off the League Championship and the UEFA Cup. The Paisley machine was on the move.

Any doubts that may have lingered about Paisley's ability, were quickly dispelled during the 1976-77 season, when he became the first English manager to lead a Football League club to the greatest European triumph of all, the European Cup. And in doing so, Paisley almost pulled off a unique treble. Liverpool won the League Championship and then at Wembley faced Manchester United in the Cup Final. It was Liverpool's chance to clinch the double and then go on to try for the classic treble. But it was not to be. United, against the run of play, pulled off a surprise 2-1 win. Within hours, Paisley had to pull his players out of the depths of despair and urge them on to a European Final in Rome. Liverpool's subsequent victory in Rome, against the German champions Borussia Moenchengladbach, was one of the finest performances from any English team in Europe and was undoubtedly a credit to his management and tactical acumen.

Bob Paisley on the pitch before extra time in the 1983 Milk Cup Final against Tottenham Hotspur, getting his players to stand up, to demonstrate that they were less tired than the opposition.

As Liverpool celebrated and their famous fans painted the Eternal City red, Paisley sat quietly and soaked in the atmosphere. 'I didn't get drunk,' he recalls. 'In fact I didn't even taste a drop. I wanted to be sober and just savour the occasion.' Thirty years earlier, Private Paisley had been part of the liberating force that had marched into Rome. Now he had returned, this time at the head of another great army, of Liverpool fans and players.

A quiet man, Bob Paisley was more at home with a cup of tea and his family than with the champagne lifestyle that had become the hallmark of far less successful managers. He sometimes even turned up at the office in his slippers, although this was because he was

troubled by an old ankle injury and the slippers made walking easier. 'He was more like a grandad,' says former defender Mark Lawrenson, 'but was probably the shrewdest person I have ever met in football.' He rarely shouted, preferring persuasion and a few quiet words in the right ear, rather than banging on tables or knocking heads together. He did sometimes lose his temper after some appalling displays, but the team's performances over the years kept such outbursts to a minimum. And when there was an outburst, it was usually left until the Monday morning rather than Saturday teatime.

Play a simple game, just pass the ball to your own man

Team talks were always short. 'We couldn't understand him anyhow,' quips Emlyn Hughes. By his own admission, Paisley was not a good communicator and Mark Lawrenson has said that at some team meetings you wondered exactly what he meant. But somehow or other his message got through, though it often had to be translated by Joe Fagan. Paisley saw football as a simple game: 'You just pass the ball to your own man. If you keep doing that you'll get yourself into a scoring position eventually. It's as easy as that.' Of course, it's not quite as simple as that but the theory at least is correct. Paisley has never been one for befriending journalists over the bar, spouting opinions or acting the expert on television. He was always polite, never on the make for money, preferring instead to let his team do the talking for him on the pitch.

The big signing – Paisley moves in for Kenny Dalglish

At the end of the 1976-77 season came Paisley's biggest test. Kevin Keegan, who had inspired Liverpool to such success on the field, was ready to quit the Merseyside club to try Continental football. Finding a replacement for the England star seemed an impossible task. It would mark the end of Liverpool, suggested some papers. But calmly and quietly, Paisley travelled to Glasgow and signed the Celtic striker Kenny Dalglish. He had been stalking Dalglish for months, never breathing a word to the press, and in the end his persistence paid off. It was to prove the greatest signing in the club's history.

The following season, Liverpool missed out on the League title but thanks to a memorable goal from Dalglish, became the first British club to win the European Cup for a second time as they beat Bruges by a single goal at Wembley. Nobody could now claim that this was Shankly's team. With Phil Neal, Dalglish,

Bob Paisley with the League Championship trophy, an award that his teams earned six times during his time in charge of Liverpool.

immortals of European soccer. Only Real Madrid had won the Cup more times than Liverpool.

And to crown his season, there was also a third trophy for the Anfield Boardroom — the Milk Cup finally captured at Maine Road against their greatest rivals, Everton. Three trophies in one season; Liverpool had finally clinched a treble, the first and only English club to have ever won three cups in one season.

A couple of weeks before their fifth European Final in 1985, Joe Fagan announced his retirement, anticipating a triumph. Instead it was to end in disaster and tears as 39 Juventus fans died in the rioting at Belgium's Heysel Stadium. Liverpool's good name in the world of soccer had been tarnished and Fagan's anticipated triumphal return turned into a nightmare. Who will ever forget the sight of the Liverpool manager struggling across the tarmac of Speke Airport, his arm wrapped around Roy Evans, tears streaming down his face as he prepared to face the press and the stunned people of the city? Since that harrowing moment, Fagan has shunned football, in an effort, perhaps, to forget the disaster that destroyed his dream.

A new departure as Dalglish becomes player-manager

The appointment of Kenny Dalglish as player-manager of Liverpool came as a genuine surprise to many closely associated with the club. It had almost been taken for granted that Ronnie Moran, as next in line, would follow the Anfield tradition by being promoted from coach to manager. But instead, Moran and his young assistant Roy Evans were bypassed in favour of Dalglish. It's long been rumoured that Dalglish was chairman John Smith's personal choice and that his selection caused a few surprises even among the directors. But John Smith knew a capable man when he saw one, and Bob Paisley had already seen the businessman in Dalglish when he said in 1982: 'Kenny calls all his goals "tap-ins" until we come to the end of the season and we are talking money. Suddenly he changes his mind.' Dalglish's success has been phenomenal, although he still has some way to go before overtaking Bob Paisley's tally of trophies and honours.

Born in Glasgow on 4 March 1951, Kenneth Mathieson Dalglish should have been an obvious target for Rangers, but instead he was snapped up by rivals Celtic where he was to enjoy outstanding success. In 240 appearances he notched up more than 100 goals and had 47 Scottish caps to his credit before Bob Paisley travelled north to sign him up. When he joined Liverpool in 1977 to replace the departing Kevin Keegan, the press speculated that it would spell major problems for Liverpool. Nobody could replace Keegan, they reckoned. Yet within a year they would have to eat their words. From his first game in a red shirt, in the Charity Shield game against Manchester United, Dalglish showed that he had a rare talent, and the

Koppites were soon describing their Scot as the finest player ever to grace the Anfield turf. And as Liverpool chairman John Smith was to say in 1986, Dalglish was 'the best player this club has signed this century.'

A season of triumph, the season of the 'double'

In his first season at Anfield, Dalglish struck 30 goals and by the end of the 1989-90 season, he could claim 172 goals in 515 contests for Liverpool. By then he was also Scotland's most capped player, with more than a century of caps, and was his country's joint leading marksman alongside Denis Law. At Anfield his success continued as he won almost every honour in the game. Even Kenny probably doesn't know how many League Championship medals are locked away in his cupboard.

But the fact remains that nobody except John Smith had the vision to foresee Dalglish's talent as a manager. Dalglish's former team-mate Graeme Souness said of him: 'Kenny was even quiet in the Liverpool team talks — or at least those team talks when the gaffer was there. He would have opinions — strong opinions, but he wouldn't offer them unless asked. But it was a different Kenny when the players were talking about conditions or whatever. In those meetings he came on like a real Govan shipyard shop steward.' Perhaps it was his determination, his will to win and his professionalism that Smith spotted and wished to nurture. Whatever it was, the talented Scot soon dispelled any lingering doubts about his ability. In his first season in charge, Liverpool clinched the double that had so often been denied them in the past. And it was fitting that Dalglish should score the goal that would see them crowned champions at Chelsea and then lead them to victory in a memorable Cup Final against their old enemy Everton.

Picking up the pieces after the Heysel disaster

No manager could have begun his career in worse circumstances, with his appointment being announced just after the Heysel tragedy. The spotlight of the world's media turned dramatically on the new man throughout the difficult weeks that followed. But if his career was to begin on such a low note, by the end of his first season he had written himself into the history books. Yet there were still criticisms of Dalglish that first season. He seemed surly in front of the TV cameras and presented a dour public image, in contrast to the usually friendly face which the club boasted. Relations with Bob Paisley were also said to be strained, with the former Liverpool

Thinking hard, Kenny Dalglish ponders the problems of management – as he could no doubt confirm, staying at the top is never easy.

54

manager quickly discarded from his advisory role. A rift between the two men was also reported and after some careless remarks to a journalist looking for some sensational copy, Paisley made a diplomatic dressing-room apology to Dalglish and his team.

Dour and difficult – Dalglish's public image

Dalglish is his own man, perhaps a little reluctant to take advice, although he listens carefully to those he respects. His relationship with the media has been strained at times though this is probably borne out of his lack of respect for Fleet Street. Instead of juicy quips for the TV cameras there was a dour, almost sharp and often non-committal response. The media in search of a quotable quote did not like it and Dalglish came in for some stern criticism. However, much of that changed after Hillsborough, when Dalglish, visibly shocked by the incident, visited the injured, asked his players to comfort the bereaved and no doubt shed tears of his own. Suddenly, Dalglish was human and his sincerity won him many more admirers among the public. 'I didn't know how much Liverpool Football Club meant to this city until Hillsborough,' he said.

Dalglish has differed in some respects from his predecessors in the boot room. He has not been afraid to go out into the transfer market and pay high prices for players he considered worthy. The old Anfield tradition of purchasing players cheaply from the lower divisions and coaching them in the reserves for 12 months, as was the Shankly and Paisley style, has continued but Dalglish has also introduced a more aggressive policy in the transfer market.

The other notable departure has been the emphasis which Dalglish has placed on attack. Previous Liverpool teams have always stressed the importance of defensive qualities. 'Get the defence right and the rest will follow,' argued Bill Shankly, and over the years Liverpool teams were always acknowledged as the most difficult to score against. It was a philosophy that certainly helped turn Liverpool into a more attractive side. Although championships and European Cups have been won in the past, there was always the accusation that Liverpool sides were dour, concentrating too much on defence. The magic that accompanied Manchester United never quite rubbed off on Liverpool until the last few years when Dalglish began to produce teams with dash and flair, committed to attack. The team that won

Together with Roy Evans (on left) Kenny Dalglish savours that champagne moment – victory 1-0 over Tottenham leads to the 1988 Barclays League Championship. He had won this title by assembling a team of remarkable flair.

the Championship in 1987-88 won applause from all quarters for its style, and was rated by Tom Finney as the finest team he had ever seen and regarded by many as the best post-war British side.

'You could win 5-0 and you might be out for the following match'

Mark Lawrenson, who served under all three recent Liverpool managers, reckons Dalglish changed the system more than any other. With Paisley and Fagan, it was always a case of choose your best 11 players, but Dalglish was more tactically aware, sometimes preferring to throw in a sweeper against certain opposition. 'The result,' says Lawrenson, 'was that you never knew if you would be playing. You could win 5-0 and you might still be out for the following match.' In other words, Dalglish played with a squad of 16 players and used them all to suit the opposition and conditions. What's more, Dalglish refused even to announce his team until the last moment — an hour before kick off — keeping players, the public, journalists and television producers all on tenterhooks.

Dalglish is dedicated – and, above all, dedicated to winning

So what makes Kenny so special? Certainly his talent on the field and his pedigree as a player have earned him enormous respect from his squad. Yet other players with similar qualifications have still failed in the managerial stakes. Above all, Dalglish is dedicated to winning. Defeat comes hard for him. As a player with Celtic and Liverpool he rarely experienced it and certainly never got used to the idea. Like his Anfield predecessors, he is not one for the high life but is essentially a quiet, sometimes even shy, family man who doesn't smoke, drink or stay out late. He is a professional in a game that at times seems to be short on players and managers who lead by example. It was that professionalism that attracted John Smith to choose him as Joe Fagan's successor and which has held him in good stead over the last five seasons.

If his success continues, then Liverpool's problem will be in holding their man to the club. He may well grow weary of the Anfield challenge and seek fresher challenges elsewhere. After all, he is still a young man. Celtic would dearly love to see him return to his roots, while Glasgow Rangers might even tempt him with a lucrative offer. But the one job which might finally tempt Kenny away from Anfield is the chance to manage his country. Almost everyone agrees, and expects, that some day Kenny will fly the fold and return to Scotland.

The fierce concentration of Kenny Dalglish is evident as he looks on anxiously during a Merseyside derby against Everton in April 1987.

BACK ROOM AND BOOT ROOM

Behind the scenes at Anfield is a wealth of experience and expertise, a team off the pitch that has an enormous amount of collective wisdom. Like so much else in the club, tradition is emphasised, and the men who prepare and choose the players have themselves often played for the club, and know exactly what the Liverpool method requires.

Rumour and speculation abound concerning the inner workings of Anfield, and people have long been asking for the secret of Liverpool's almost unending success, and no doubt there are several answers. One, for instance, is their refusal ever to give up until the final whistle has sounded. Another is their approach when it comes to management and the back room team: they firmly believe in sticking to traditions, and staying with the devil they know. While some clubs hire and fire man-

agers at the drop of a hat, Liverpool, in almost a century of their history, have had no more than a dozen team bosses. In the past 30 years, they have had just four. The first of this quartet, Bill Shankly, who joined the club in December 1959, was, according to his successor Bob Paisley, 'the best brain-washer I've ever encountered.' And *that* was meant as a compliment!

In the beginning, Bill Shankly was aided by a fellow-Scot called Reuben Bennett, an ex-Army physical training instructor and professional goalkeeper. They used to tell the story of Reuben having taken the longest goal kick in the history of the game: when he kicked the ball, it went out of the ground, landed on a lorry and travelled all the way to Carlisle. But Reuben wasn't employed as Liverpool's goalkeeper, he was their trainer.

Having assessed his playing side, Shanks dispensed with the services of two dozen players, but he kept faith with the back room staff. He made his demands crystal-clear when it came to the back room side: loyalty to each other, as well as to himself, and no back-biting.

Shanks preached the gospel of collective effort

The one thing that mattered most of all was that everyone should pull together in the cause of Liverpool. And this has been the story ever since. Shanks preached the gospel of collective effort, with everyone working for and with each other. And while the team kicked the ball around on the field of play, the boys in the back room kicked around ideas designed to further the cause of Liverpool Football Club.

Since Shanks's departure from the club after their 1974 FA Cup success, Liverpool have 'kept it in the family' when it comes to appointing the men whose job it is to oversee the players. Bob Paisley arrived as a young hopeful when he joined Liverpool in May 1939, and he stayed to serve the club for more than half a century in various roles — player, trainer, physiotherapist, coach, assistant to the manager, manager and director. As Bob Paisley stepped up as successor to Shankly, so did other back room boys: Joe Fagan, Ronnie Moran and Roy Evans. When Bob stepped down, he handed over the reins to Joe Fagan, and when Joe decided to retire, Kenny Dalglish — a Liverpool player of several years' standing — was given the job.

The Anfield boot room has become famous throughout the world of football as a place where hospitality is dispensed to opposite numbers from the visiting clubs. You came, you played your game expecting nothing in the way of charity, but once the match was over you were made welcome in the boot room, to have a quiet

The boot room itself, repository of the wisdom of ages, here embodied in the form of (from left) Kenny Dalglish, Ronnie Moran and Roy Evans. Their experience stretches back decades. Nowhere can there be more informed conversation about the game.

drink and chat with the back room men there. And on Sunday mornings, the Liverpool staff would gather in the boot room to weigh up all that had happened in matches played by the various teams the day before.

Switching from the playing side to the coaching side

Sunday morning was the time for offering opinions, after a cooling-off period of almost 24 hours; a time when everyone was entitled to say his piece, when people could and did disagree with each other — but, all the while, the object of the exercise was to eliminate past mistakes and ensure that Liverpool prospered in the future. That 'brain-washing', to which Bob Paisley referred, lingers on too, because down the corridor from the boot room, just where the respective teams go out of the dressing-rooms and make their way towards the entrance to the playing area, there is a plaque on the wall saying: 'This is Anfield'. It's calculated to inspire the Liverpool players and give the opposition cause to harbour doubts about themselves.

The illustrious roll-call of back room staff at Anfield — Bill Shankly, Bob Paisley, Reuben Bennett, Joe Fagan, Ronnie Moran, Roy Evans, Tom Saunders, Phil Thompson, Ron Yeats, Geoff Twentyman, Steve Heighway, John Bennison, Hughie McAuley — is very impressive, and in most instances, these men played for Liverpool before switching to the back room side of the game. Between them, they have experienced just about every facet of football, from talent-spotting missions to coaching youngsters, assessing the opposition at home and abroad, working out tactics and ensuring that players are fit enough for the demanding roles they are asked to play on the park.

Connections and friendships that go back a long way

Bob Paisley arrived at Anfield after having played for the famed non-League club Bishop Auckland. Joe Fagan, who was in charge of the reserves during his early days with Liverpool, played for Manchester City and Bradford Park Avenue before becoming player-manager of non-Leaguers Nelson, and then manager at Anfield. He served in the Navy during the Second World War, and was a Combined Services team-mate of Tom Saunders, an Army man, when their paths crossed during the war in the Middle East.

Tom Saunders, a Liverpudlian, spent close on 30 years in the teaching profession, the last three as a headmaster. He also made his mark as a manager of schoolboy football teams — 10 years as the team boss of the England schoolboy side and a spell managing the Under-18 professional international team. In 1970, when he was 49, Liverpool invited him to give up his teaching job and become involved full-time in football.

ABOVE: Steve Heighway in action in 1976 and (LEFT) in the role of Youth Development Officer that he took on later.

Some people thought — and said — that he was mad to accept. But he couldn't resist the challenge, and when Liverpool asked him what he wanted to be called, he came up with the title of 'Youth Development Officer'. He was the first in the game, and many other clubs have since followed suit. Tom had an unassuming honesty about the way that he talked to young players about their career chances, and earned respect for not making outrageous promises.

In his early days at Anfield, Tom's job was coaching youngsters and, when the time came to persuade them to sign, talking to them and their parents. As the years passed, his job broadened out so that he went talent-spotting and checking out the opposition, especially when Liverpool were playing in the European Cup. Tom would pack his bags and depart for foreign climes, returning with an in-depth dossier on the team Liverpool were due to meet. This one-time manager of the Liverpool schoolboys' side — he was also an FA staff

coach — officially retired a few years ago, but there is still a welcome for Tom Saunders at Anfield, and on match days they make room for him to sit in the dug-out, alongside Chief Coach Ronnie Moran, First Team Assistant Coach Roy Evans and Kenny Dalglish, although Kenny is usually to be seen on his feet.

Roy Evans: learning to coach by winning with the reserves

Like Tom Saunders, Roy Evans and Ronnie Moran are Liverpool-born, though their careers contrasted sharply as players. Roy, a former England schoolboy international, made fewer than a dozen senior appearances as full-back between the 1969-70 season and 1973-74, and he was still only in his mid-20s when he was persuaded to switch to the coaching side. When he took charge of the reserves, they achieved a hat-trick of Central

League Championships, finished a fourth term as runners-up, collected the title again during the next four seasons, and later claimed two more Championship successes. Then Roy was promoted, to work with the seniors alongside Ronnie Moran.

Ronnie Moran: letting the players know what he thinks

Ronnie has spent close on 40 years at the club, graduating from player to senior first-team coach. And the 17-year-old Moran was recommended to Liverpool in the first instance by a local postman who delivered mail to the home of a club director. He won't thank you for reminding him that when he made his first-team debut, away against Derby County, Liverpool lost 3-2. But he stayed in the side and, during five seasons, he missed only half a dozen matches. His career stretched from the 1952-53 season to 1964-65, so as well as claiming a Championship medal in the 1963-64 season, he was

in at the start of Liverpool's European saga. He packed one of the hardest shots in the game, scored goals from the penalty spot, and totalled 379 senior appearances before turning his attention to coaching. For many years, Ronnie was in charge of the reserve team and the young Kevin Keegan recalled sampling the strength of Moran's displeasure when he was given a dressing down: 'I went into the dressing-room at half-time once, and Ronnie Moran immediately started on me: "What the hell do you think you are doing? You're not playing like a Liverpool player," he said. "What do you mean?" I said, completely taken aback. "You're just free and easy," he replied. "You are just charging about the midfield. You're nearly playing up front. You're a midfield player with defensive responsibilities." For a while I felt disillusioned. Now that I know Ronnie, I realise he was trying to help me.'

The same can be said about another Liverpudlian, Phil Thompson, who captained club and country. And although Phil did have a brief spell with Sheffield United when his playing career came to a close at Anfield, it

BELOW: Ron Yeats as successful captain in the 1960s and (RIGHT) as successful scout in the 1980s.

wasn't long before he was being asked to return, this time to take charge of the reserves.

Phil made his League debut for Liverpool in the 1971-72 season, and that was the start of a dozen seasons of active service which saw him claiming no fewer than seven League-Championship medals, as well as winner's medals in various Cup competitions. Phil played in midfield or in defence, was a member of the victorious 1974 FA Cup Final team, and won two European Cup medals and a UEFA Cup medal. Capped 42 times by England, he also made more than 460 appearances for Liverpool.

Steve Heighway: from flying winger to Youth Development Officer

Another member of the coaching staff who played more than 460 games for the club is Steve Heighway, and this former Anfield favourite is now the club's Youth Development Officer, working alongside Youth Team Coach John Bennison and the latest recruit, Hughie

Ronnie Moran looking calm, but probably wondering which player needs the edge of his tongue to really get him going. He attends to most details about the way that the players approach the game, and works on technical points.

McAuley. While Heighway graduated to stardom via amateur football with Skelmersdale United, Bennison played non-League Soccer in Wales and with South Liverpool, and McAuley moved on from Anfield to Plymouth Argyle and Tranmere Rovers. So far as Heighway, Bennison and McAuley are concerned, the accent is very much on developing a good youth system that will put players through to the first team.

The finest amateur footballer Bob Paisley had ever seen

Heighway is ideally suited to follow in the footsteps of Tom Saunders because, while he has an academic background, he knows all the pitfalls in the game which can await a star-struck youngster. Heighway graduated from university with a Bachelor of Arts degree and, at that time, it seemed his career might lie in teaching. But his displays for Skelmersdale had brought him to the attention of Liverpool. Bob Paisley recalls how his sons, Robert and Graham, first told him about the high-stepping winger, and so he went along to take a look for

himself. Bob saw Steve taking the South Liverpool defence apart, and on his return to Anfield he told Tony Waiters, who was then on the coaching staff, that Heighway was the finest amateur footballer he had seen. Waiters went to have a look, too, and was equally impressed. The upshot was that Steve was persuaded to take his chance on a career in football, though at the back of his mind there was the thought that he could always turn to teaching. He made his League debut in the 1970-71 season, became a regular through 10 more campaigns, and totalled 76 goals in his 467 appearances.

From captain to Chief Scout – Geoff Twentyman and Ron Yeats

Steve was by no means certain that he could last the pace as a professional, but he proved himself and other doubters wrong. He once confessed that it was an Anfield derby game against Everton that really brought home to him what playing for Liverpool, and being a true professional, meant. Liverpool, two goals down, managed to draw level and, in the final stages of the game, snatch a winner. It was then, as he saw the reaction of team-mates who were Liverpool-born and bred, that it hit Steve Heighway just what winning a derby game was all about. And when he left Anfield to play for Minnesota Kicks, in the United States Soccer League, he made it clear that, having played for Liverpool, there was no other club in this country which could have tempted him.

When he did return to England, it was at the invitation of the Anfield club. Once again, Liverpool were keeping it in the family as they gave Steve the chance to become Youth Development Officer. And similarly, another one-time Liverpool hero returned to take on a new role. He was Ron Yeats, who succeeded Geoff Twentyman — yet again a former Liverpool player — as Chief Scout.

Twentyman had kicked off as an 18-year-old footballer with Carlisle United — one of the clubs that Bill Shankly had managed before he joined Liverpool. In December 1953, Twentyman became a Liverpool player, after almost 150 games for the Cumbrian club, and during seven seasons at Anfield he totalled close on 200 first-team appearances. He left in the first term of Shankly's management and became player-manager of Ballymena United, in the Irish League.

In June 1963, Geoff Twentyman rejoined Carlisle, but eventually he returned to Liverpool, whom he had skippered for a brief spell, taking on the role of Chief Scout. After his departure from Anfield, it was Graeme Souness, an ex-Liverpool hero, who signed him up in a similar role for Glasgow Rangers. Meanwhile, Liverpool's Scottish clan was bolstered when Big Ron Yeats, a key player during the Shankly regime, was appointed by Kenny Dalglish as Chief Scout. Aberdeen-born Yeats arrived at Anfield from Dundee United in July

1961, and after his £30,000 signing, he was introduced by Shanks to the press as 'a colossus'. This giant certainly made an impression, as he stayed at Anfield for 10 years and totalled more than 450 first-team games. Indeed, he became the first Liverpool captain to walk up the steps at Wembley and collect the FA Cup. He captained Liverpool also to the League Championship on two occasions, and when he hung up his boots with the club, he moved the short distance to Tranmere Rovers, who signed the big man up as their player-manager.

A Swedish view: the attention to detail is all-important

Towards the end of the 1980s, Ron Yeats was back on home territory as he became Liverpool's Chief Scout, and in this role he travels thousands of miles a year, checking on potential signings. He also does another job, from time to time — and this is an indication of the attention Liverpool pay to the finer details. Often, when several players are appearing in a home international, Ron will be at the match. When it's over, he'll chauffeur the players back to Merseyside. That way, they're back in their own beds during the early hours of the morning and, if need be, they can go in to Anfield for treatment without delay.

Liverpool have not hesitated to buy big when they felt the occasion demanded it, and one of their most recent signings, Swedish international Glenn Hysen, who captained his country during the 1990 World Cup Finals, has offered some interesting thoughts about the Anfield club, and what makes it tick: 'After the first couple of training sessions, I began to realise why Liverpool are such a great club. They pay attention to the smallest detail, and when someone is injured there is always another player ready to slot into the side. I realised another thing, too. While you may feel you're watching a team of stars when Liverpool appear on television, when you get close up to them you find that everyone — back room staff and players — has to keep his feet firmly on the ground. There simply is no star system.'

Last season is always past history. The next season is what matters

Hysen became the first Swedish player to claim a League-Championship medal in the English First Division, and it meant a great deal to him, even though he had won a UEFA Cup medal twice with Gothenburg and had also enjoyed the experience of playing for two other top Continental clubs, PSV Eindhoven and Fiorentina. In Hysen's opinion, the English First Division is the toughest League of all. But Hysen has already learned enough about the boot room boys to realise that so far as Liverpool are concerned, last season's triumph is something to enjoy for a brief moment —

then you forget it. It's a lesson every player has learned, and one that the men on the back room staff never allow you to forget. Nor, of course, do they ever forget it themselves.

'The boot room is to a football club what the boiler room is to a luxury liner'

All the players who pulled on the red shirt of Liverpool during the 1980s owed something to the men in the boot room. Craig Johnston, one of the heroes of the 'double' year, once said: 'The boot room may smell of polish, sweat and leather. But the boot room is to a football club what the boiler room is to a luxury liner: a dark inner sanctum off-limits to the public, where the real power that drives the colossus comes from. All the boot room staff, from Fagan to Ronnie Moran, were ex-players steeped in the Shankly philosophy.' Liverpool have set the standard for themselves and for all their rivals, and in setting those standards, the men in the

Phil Thompson came back to the club as reserve-team coach only 18 months after he stopped playing for Liverpool in 1985.

back room have been as much a part of the overall pattern as the players who perform on the park on a Saturday afternoon.

Information, knowledge and years of collective experience

What this background strength gives Liverpool is information going back a long way and tested by years of practical experience of the way the Football League works. About the way individual players perform, about the way certain combinations of players perform. About what seems to work at certain times of year and about how certain skills that can look very good on firm grounds as a season opens may become valueless as the heavy winter pitches change the way the game is played. The fanatical attention to detail that the boot room boys lived by was not lost on the players. In the early 1970s, Kevin Keegan described how: 'Liverpool

The Anfield dressing room in November 1987, and Liverpool prepare to take on Watford in an evening match. While Steve McMahon (on right) looks tense (although he went on to score in the match), John Barnes seems to be relishing the contest against the club he had recently left. He was also on the scoresheet that night. Peter Beardsley (on left) also looks relaxed and confident, perhaps because of something that Kenny Dalglish (standing with back to camera) has said. RIGHT: Ronnie Moran works on Alan Hansen's calves before the same match.

have a book which the players refer to as the "Bible". Shanks started it and Joe Fagan now keeps it. It contains most of the secrets of Liverpool's success, showing what the team does every day of every week of every year. Our approach to training from pre-season to the final match was logged. If we made a mistake, it was there in black and white for everyone to see. If we produced a winning formula, it was also there for reference. I would often hear Joe say, "That's funny. Three years ago a similar problem cropped up, and there's the answer in the book."'

Keeping it professional, keeping it behind the scenes

So Liverpool's coaching and scouting team is closely knit, and the majority of its members know the club inside out because they've been through the mill there as players. They know what's expected of them and they know how to put the message across to the players who have followed in their footsteps. If it was Bill Shankly who set the pattern more than 30 years ago, it was people such as Bob Paisley, Joe Fagan, Ronnie Moran and Roy Evans who made sure it was repeated season after season. And the other members of the back room staff have been and remain completely in tune with the club's requirements.

There is one final point that is also critical. The men who serve behind the scenes at Anfield have been part of an enormously successful machine, but few of them wish to leave it, to manage a club on their own. They are very happy to go about their job in a professional manner, producing the best team in the Football League without demanding personal fame. Indeed, in the case of Joe Fagan, and perhaps also Bob Paisley, there was a positive dislike of the limelight. Professionalism and hard work bring these men great personal satisfaction, and they would rather know they are doing a good job than be feted in the fickle spotlight of fame.

ABOVE: Aldridge wishes Barnes luck minutes before kick-off against Watford. John Aldridge, too, scored in the ensuing 4-0 victory.

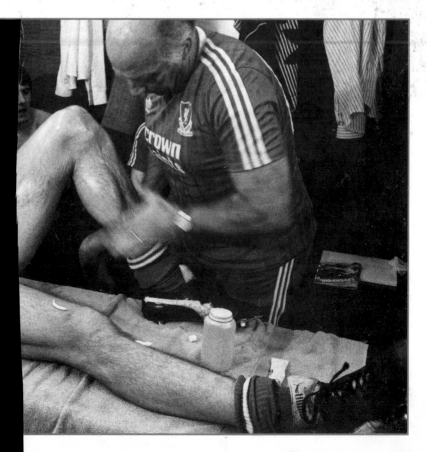

HEYSEL

At the Heysel Stadium in Brussels on 29 May 1985, Liverpool were bidding to become the first team since Real Madrid to win three European Cups in a row. And then, in that swelteringly hot evening, disaster struck. Some of the club's own supporters led an attack on Juventus fans, and a wall collapsed. Thirty-nine people died, and over 400 were injured.

Players and fans alike expected Wednesday 29 May 1985 to be another night of triumph and glory for Liverpool Football Club, but it ended in slaughter and trauma.

Liverpool's hopes were high as they prepared to face Juventus in the Final of the European Cup in the Heysel Stadium in Brussels. But before a ball had been kicked it turned into a nightmare that resulted in 39 deaths and more than 400 injuries, most suffered by Juventus fans. A world-wide television audience of 400 million had tuned in expecting to watch a classic confrontation between the champions of Italy and England, between Paolo Rossi and Michel Platini and Ian Rush and Kenny Dalglish. Instead, they were horrified to watch rampaging Liverpool fans tearing down the wire mesh that separated them from their Italian 'enemies' on the terrace in Block Z. The terrified Italian fans ran for their lives, but reached a dead-end. When a wall gave way, hundreds were crushed under the sheer weight of the stampeding, panic-stricken crowd.

'Those poor bloody Italians went down like a pack of cards'

A core of Liverpool 'fans' were responsible for the deaths of innocent people. They had made three charges that sent the Italians fleeing under a barrage of iron rods, rocks, kicks and punches. The final charge ended in mass slaughter. As one off-duty British policeman put it: 'Those poor bloody Italians went down like a pack of cards. The metal railings just folded under their combined weight.' There were strong criticisms of the Belgian police. Although more than 1000 police and paramilitary gendarmes were on duty at the stadium before the match — which increased to over 2,300 when reinforcements were called in — not a single Briton was arrested by the police during the murderous rioting. Only nine Britons were in custody and they had been arrested in the sporadic outbreaks of violence and theft that preceded the game.

In their defence, the Belgian police were concerned above all in restoring order among the 58,000-strong crowd. The police even had to arrest a Moroccan for stealing from the pockets of the corpses. Until ambulances got to the scene 30 minutes after the riot began, the dead and injured were covered with team flags and carried out of the stadium on crowd control barriers.

Playing the game to avoid further crowd violence

Another immediate controversy was whether the match should have gone ahead. Jacques Georges, President of UEFA, described how he had gone to the Juventus dressing room to speak to the captain, Michel Platini: 'The player asked, "Mr Georges, people have died outside. How many?" I said "I don't know." Platini said, "You don't want to tell me." I said "no".' Realising that much of the crowd was unaware of the magnitude of the tragedy and fearful of triggering an even more terrible riot, UEFA officials and the Belgian police decided th[...] manager Jo[...] loudspeake[...] Liverpool l[...] Michel Plati[...]

What [...]

When the pl[...] they made [...] about what [...] season with[...] fans telling [...] don't think [...] spoke of hi[...] professiona[...]

Belgian po[...] **heart of an**[...] **wall collap**[...] criticised c[...] observers [...] too lax, bu[...] behaviour[...]

appeared as a substitute for Paul Walsh in the second half, said 'We had to play to prevent further trouble. It was very difficult to do.'

'Only the English fans were responsible. Of that there is no doubt'

Ian Rush, who later joined Juventus, said 'There had been a warm-up game on the pitch beforehand involving local Belgian lads, and we were told that they had been killed. They were just young boys, about 15. That upset us most of all. We heard all sorts of stories. Someone said a couple had died, someone said 40. We had to try to forget because there was a job to do on the pitch, but you can't do that. It wasn't a cup final.'

In the week after Heysel a tremendous row erupted about who exactly was to blame for the disaster. Jacques Georges had no doubts: 'Victims went to Brussels to celebrate the match of the century. They were not able to return home. They were the victims of a barbaric action by Liverpool fans that we all condemn.' Mr Gunter Schneider of West Germany, the official UEFA observer at the game, agreed: 'Only the English fans were responsible. Of that there is no doubt.' UEFA's secretary, Hans Bangeuter, rejected claims that stadium security and policing were inadequate. He said: 'Had the spectators behaved themselves, there would not have been danger at all. It is not the state of the stadium which is responsible, it was the action of the so-called Liverpool spectators who must take the blame for this outrageous tragedy.'

UEFA takes the decision to ban English clubs indefinitely

While there was plenty of outraged reaction in Britain there was a suspicion among foreign commentators that it was superficial. Unlike the French and Italian, the British Embassy in Brussels sent no wreath to the service for the bereaved. Nor did Liverpool Football Club. Meanwhile, the European football authorities were evolving a harsh punishment for English football. Louis Wouters, President of the Belgian Football Federation, said the day after the disaster: 'We must be finished with those people who come to kill, steal and destroy.' On 2 June, Jacques Georges, UEFA's president, announced that English football clubs would be banned from taking part in European competition 'for an indeterminate period of time', and that Liverpool would face an additional ban of three years on top of that.

LEFT: After the excesses of some Liverpool fans, the hooligan element among the Juventus supporters showed their feelings, if not their faces. RIGHT: Rescuers carry out the dead and injured on makeshift stretchers, while the shocked crowd looks on, scarcely able to believe what has happened.

THEIR EXPRESSIONS OF JOY OR OUT THEIR DUTIE
DISAPPOINTMENT WITHIN THE LIMITS UNRULY MINORIT
OF NORMAL GOOD SPORTING ENJOYMENT OF T
BEHAVIOUR — HELP THE STADIUM HAVE COME TO S
SECURITY OFFICIALS IN CARRYING UEFA THANKS YO

For Liverpool, a club that had graced European competitions for over 20 years, the decision was terrible. The club attempted to fight the ban. On 8 August 1985, a UEFA Board of Appeal met in Switzerland to discuss the appeal by Liverpool against the additional three year ban. Liverpool Director and legal representative Tony Ensor, along with Peter Robinson, presented a 132 page document detailing 'new evidence' on the disaster. The board decided that the evidence did not merit a reduction in the penalty. Liverpool captain Phil Neal condemned the decision. He said: 'I am totally stunned. I feel it is part of a cover up by UEFA to save their own necks. It has been proved that the Belgian police were at fault so how can they put all the blame on our club? I think UEFA have got to look

supporters were eventually convicted of manslaughter by a Belgian court in 1989. They were given sentences of three years. On appeal in 1990, seven had their sentences increased by one year, four had their sentences increased by two years, while one other was cleared of the original charges. Only one of those originally convicted was in court for the appeal hearing. To the end of the decade, the others faced extradition to serve their sentences. Summing up, the judge said one of the reasons the sentences had been stiffened was the fans' clear lack of remorse.

The Heysel Stadium disaster, for good reason, should not be allowed to slip out of popular memory. It was the blackest point in the history of Liverpool Football Club, and the guilty fans brought shame and

ABOVE: Joe Fagan on the left of the bench, had hoped to end his career at the top, having won a fifth European Cup for Liverpool. Instead, he returned home with his dream turned to ashes, signing off in the wake of a disaster.

RIGHT: Antonio Cabrini of Juventus pleads with Italian fans to try to persuade them to calm down. A mass confrontation and rioting on an even bigger scale appeared a distinct possibility at this stage, with the Italian fans in a state of outrage.

at themselves. To pick a venue like the Heysel Stadium was an error of judgement. Right now I am devastated'.

For Jacques Georges, the appeal fell on deaf ears, as he explained: 'UEFA is ready to take any action necessary to deal with the violence that is killing our sport. Now there are no more small incidents. Everything will be punished. We owe this to the memory of the dead.'

After lengthy extradition procedures 14 Liverpool

dishonour to English football. The subsequent years have demonstrated the damage that the European ban has done to English football. Heysel had shamed the club in the eyes of the world. For Liverpool manager Joe Fagan it was the saddest night of his distinguished career. He had wished that in his last match in charge of Liverpool he could triumph and bring home the European Cup. But he returned instead with burning shame and a bowed head.

DOUBLE TRIUMPH

After the Heysel disaster and the resignation of Joe Fagan, many observers wondered whether the Liverpool side could pick itself up and make a challenge for titles in the 1985-86 season. This speculation became even more intense when the Board appointed their new manager – and sprang a real surprise by choosing Kenny Dalglish.

On 5 October 1985, Manchester United were held to a 1-1 draw at Luton Town, ending a sequence of 10 consecutive League victories. United, however, faded as the Championship race hotted up, and Liverpool, who had started the season poorly came from behind in both the Championship race and the FA Cup Final, and triumphantly achieved the classic Soccer double. Liverpool had proved once again that the essential ingredient in title-winning is consistency. However, there were occasions when the Anfield Reds themselves appeared to be wilting — especially when they came up against Manchester United and Everton in the League. On 22 February 1986, they lost 2-0 at Anfield to Everton — the team Bill Shankly used to call 'the other team' on Merseyside. After the game, Everton's captain, Kevin Ratcliffe, said: 'It was not the Liverpool we are used to seeing. I don't know what they were trying to do, and I don't think they knew either.'

But as the final weeks of the season went by, Liverpool strung together a run of results which took them through 18 matches — all without defeat — during March, April, and the last 10 days of the campaign, in May. In the end, they finished two points ahead of Everton, four in front of third-placed West Ham, and a dozen points ahead of Manchester United, who finished in fourth place.

In August, Liverpool reeled off victories over Arsenal and Ipswich Town (5-0), but draws with Aston Villa and West Ham, and defeat at St James's Park against Newcastle on the 24 August, left them in 18th position. Liverpool began to pick up in September — they played seven games and won six of them — notably the derby game against Everton, which they won 3-2 with goals from Dalglish, Rush and McMahon.

By the end of the month, with 10 League games

gone, Liverpool had climbed to second place in the table — but they were still nine points adrift of Manchester United, who had won all their matches and scored 27 goals while conceding only three. Even at that stage, some people were ready to award the Championship prize to Ron Atkinson's men. But not Liverpool, and not Ian Rush, who had already bagged eight goals by the end of September.

The race begins with Manchester United making all the running

As October began, Manchester United were still leading the pack, with 38 points from 14 matches, while Liverpool lagged 10 points behind. In October, Liverpool lost to Queen's Park Rangers, but gained League wins over Southampton and Luton. They had also prised a valuable point out of Manchester United in the Old Trafford League duel, with Craig Johnston the marksman. By the end of November, only two points separated Liverpool and United.

Liverpool were beginning to knit together. Ian Rush had taken his tally to a dozen. And Paul Walsh was also figuring regularly on the scoresheet, including scoring two goals against his old club, Luton, a hat-trick against Brighton, and goals in successive games against Coventry, West Brom and Birmingham.

Liverpool knew, however, that while they had closed the gap between themselves and United, they could not afford to be as generous as they had been against Chelsea at Anfield, where they had let a 1-0 lead slip away in the dying minutes. Chelsea, like West Ham, had emerged as title challengers — the Hammers were third, Chelsea fourth, Wednesday fifth and Everton sixth, nine points adrift of Manchester United, as the last month of the year loomed. And for Liverpool, December was an unhappy month: they won only two of their half-dozen matches, and towards the end of the month they had slipped to fourth spot, with United, Chelsea and Everton above them.

PLayer-manager Kenny Dalglish and goalkeeper Bruce Grobbelaar enjoy the 3-1 FA Cup triumph over Everton that gave them the 'double'. They were only the third club this century to perform this feat.

As the clubs entered January, they also took on the challenge of winning the FA Cup. For Liverpool, this meant that they had seven games during the month, because they also had a Milk Cup-tie against Ipswich Town and the Screen Sport Super Cup return against Spurs. Liverpool kicked off the New Year by drawing 2-2 with Sheffield Wednesday and dispatching Norwich City from the FA Cup competition, with a 5-0 victory in their third-round tie. Then they beat Watford 3-2, Spurs 3-0, West Ham 3-1 and — in the fifth round of the Milk Cup — Ipswich Town 3-0. The last match of the month was the fourth-round FA Cup-tie against Chelsea, and it brought Liverpool a 2-1 victory. Ian Rush, by then, was leading the way as a marksman, with 19 goals in all competitions, while Paul Walsh added to his haul by scoring in five of the games during January.

Into February, and Everton take up the leader's position

February was significant for the fact that, for the first time, the leadership of the First Division changed hands — at long last, it seemed as if Manchester United had been cut down to size. But it wasn't Liverpool who overhauled them at the top — it was Everton who led the way on the first day of the month. February was a testing month for Liverpool, who faced some tricky encounters, especially in the Cup competitions. Liverpool drew 1-1 with Norwich in the first leg of their Screen Sport Super Cup semi-final, and were indebted to John Wark for a point-saver against Manchester United. Liverpool then lost 1-0 in the first leg of their Milk Cup semi-final against Queen's Park Rangers. And in the fifth round of the FA Cup against York City, Liverpool had to settle for a draw and an Anfield replay.

In the return game against York, Liverpool won 3-1, but in their final game of the month, they fell 2-0 as they lost to Everton at Anfield. So it was Everton at the top, with 56 points from 28 matches, Liverpool in fourth spot (53 points from 28 games). Manchester United had 55 points, Chelsea 54 and both these clubs had two matches in hand. Things got worse, rather than better, during the early days of March, because Everton improved their position at the expense of both Liverpool and Manchester United.

First disappointment: losing in the Milk Cup semi-final

Liverpool had nine matches during March, and it was during this month that their Championship challenge began to pick up pace. They started with a 2-1 victory against Spurs at White Hart Lane. However, they were

Mark Lawrenson's consistency was critical during a season in which Liverpool were often below their best, but still came away with satisfactory results.

left feeling sorry for themselves when they failed to beat Queen's Park Rangers in their Milk Cup semi-final return at Anfield. Steve McMahon and Craig Johnston got their names on the scoresheet for the home side, but Rangers struck twice, to take the tie on a 3-2 aggregate and ensure that they, and not Liverpool, marched on to Wembley. There was to be no treble!

Kenny Dalglish didn't duck the issue after the match — he admitted that he and his players were bitterly disappointed by the setback, but in typical Liverpool fashion he offered the opinion that his team would carry on doing its best to win the next match, which was in the League against QPR, three days later. And the Liverpool players certainly shrugged off their Milk Cup blues as they put four goals past Rangers, while conceding one. Steve McMahon was a two-goal man, with Ian Rush and John Wark hitting the other goals.

By this stage of the season, of course, the FA Cup was beginning to loom as a major prize, as well as the Championship, and both the Merseyside giants were still on course for Wembley. Liverpool's Cup run had kicked off on a grey day in January as snowflakes swept across Anfield and it needed a referee's inspection before the tie against Norwich City could get under way. Five goals saw off the Canaries, and in the fourth round — a tie televised live on the Sunday afternoon — goals from Ian Rush and Mark Lawrenson had put paid to Chelsea at Stamford Bridge.

The FA Cup campaign – replay after replay

In the fifth-round tie at York, Liverpool had come from behind after Gary Ford had put City in the driving seat. Four minutes later, a disputed penalty gave Jan Molby the chance to level the score, and he made no mistake. In the Anfield replay, the score stood at 1-1 after 90 minutes, but Liverpool edged ahead in extra time, to win 3-1. In mid-March, they faced a sixth-round meeting with Graham Taylor's Watford. At Anfield, his team gave such a good account of themselves that they kept Liverpool scoreless, and this meant a Vicarage Road replay. A superb John Barnes free-kick, which ended up in the back of the Liverpool net, seemed likely to earn The Hornets a semi-final place. But in the dying minutes of the match, Liverpool were awarded a penalty, and Jan Molby once more showed that he could be spot-on from the spot. Extra time brought the goal that won the tie, and it came from Ian Rush.

Also through were Southampton, Sheffield Wednesday and Everton. But the luck of the draw kept the Merseyside clubs apart — it was Liverpool versus Southampton at White Hart Lane, with Everton and Wednesday clashing at Villa Park. So the prospect of an historic, all-Merseyside Final still dangled enticingly for Liverpool and Everton.

In the meantime, though, the battle for the League Championship was entering a crucial stage as well, and in between their two Cup-ties against Watford, Liverpool beat Southampton 2-1, then they went to town against Oxford United, hammering them 6-0. Maurice Evans, then manager of Oxford, said before the match: 'Playing at Anfield will be a new experience for almost all of my lads. I don't know if any of them will feel overawed by the occasion, but it will certainly teach them something!' The last match in March, a month in which they had remained undefeated, brought a 2-0 win over Manchester City, and that success — Steve McMahon struck both goals — took Liverpool to the top of the First Division for the first time during the campaign. It was Easter Monday, and that day, also, Everton and Manchester United were figuring in a scoreless draw at Old Trafford. So it was Liverpool with 70 points from 36 matches, just sufficient to put them ahead of Everton on goal difference, though the Blues still had a game in hand. As for United, they trailed by five points, after having played three dozen games.

The FA Cup semi-finals lead to a Merseyside Final

On 5 April, both Liverpool and Everton were engaged on FA Cup business, and Manchester United took advantage of this to narrow the gap in the League, as they won 3-1 at Coventry, though Chelsea — still trying to make an impact — lost ground as they dropped points at home to Ipswich Town. However, it was the Cup which concerned both Liverpool and Everton on Saturday 5 April 1986, and while the men from Merseyside were favourites in each case, they were made to battle every inch of the way — so much so, that both of the matches went to extra time. After 90 minutes at White Hart Lane there was still no score, while the situation at Villa Park was a 1-1 stalemate between Everton and Wednesday. But seven minutes into extra time, Graeme Sharp struck for Everton; and two minutes later, in the other semi-final, it was Ian Rush who broke the deadlock between Liverpool and the Saints. Five minutes after that, the Welsh international scored his second goal. So, the 'dream' Final had become a reality, with Liverpool and Everton to meet in an FA Cup Final at Wembley for the first time in the history of the two clubs.

Yet before this glamorous occasion, there was still the business of the League Championship to be settled, and Liverpool began to make further headway in the League.

They followed up their semi-final success by rattling in five goals without any reply from Coventry City, and then beat Luton Town, West Brom, Birmingham City (another 5-0 drubbing) and Leicester City. Ronnie Whelan had scored a hat-trick against the Sky Blues, and Gary Gillespie achieved a similar feat against Birmingham. Ian Rush, meanwhile, had taken his haul for the season to 31 goals.

The season was building up to a sensational climax

as Everton won at Watford and Manchester United won at Newcastle, while Liverpool were beating Luton Town; and, not to be outdone, West Ham came back into the Championship frame with a run of victories. It all meant that, four games in the space of eight days decided that the League championship and the FA Cup were destined to rest on the Anfield sideboard.

Everton and West Ham take the contest to the last Saturday of the League

As the last Saturday of the League season dawned, Liverpool, Everton and West Ham were still in contention, although the Anfield Reds knew that their fate was in their own hands. They had to travel to Stamford Bridge and take on Chelsea, and if they could win that one, the Championship would be theirs — but they hadn't won there since 1974. If they drew or lost that day, then it could all hinge on what Everton and West Ham could achieve.

Everton were playing Southampton at Goodison Park, the Hammers had to take on West Brom at The Hawthorns — and then, 48 hours later, in the final fixture of the season, Everton were to play West Ham at Goodison Park.

And on Saturday 3 May 1986, Everton certainly did their best to upset the odds, because they hammered half a dozen goals past the hapless Saints, with Gary Lineker hitting a hat-trick. It was a do-or-die attempt by the Blues to catch up on goal difference, as well as points. At The Hawthorns, West Ham cruised into a two-goal lead, then allowed West Brom to battle back and draw level with a penalty goal, shortly after an hour's play. Six minutes later, though, full-back Ray Stewart stepped up to slot home his third spot-kick goal in as many matches, and the Hammers had the points in the bag. Both theirs and Everton's efforts, however, had all been in vain: Liverpool had scored the one goal which really counted.

Clinching the League title against Chelsea

The man who rifled the all-important goal was player-manager Kenny Dalglish, and that goal was sufficient not only to win the match, but to clinch the League Championship. This game against Chelsea was far from a classic. Chelsea were determined not to do Liverpool any favours, and the poor playing surface did not

Paul Walsh brings the ball down with his chest. Walsh and Dalglish were Rush's main striking partners during this 'double' season, with Walsh (who scored 11 goals in a 17-match mid-season spell) taking much of the pressure off Dalglish, who was able to save himself for the vital Championship run-in, including the crucial last game.

encourage flowing football. Some of the physical challenges were fearsome, and Craig Johnston finished the game with a bloody nose after a clash with Rougvie, the tough Scots defender playing for the London side. Dalglish's goal was beautifully taken, however: Jim Beglin hit the ball towards the manager, who controlled it on his chest before hitting a curling volley that delighted his team-mates.

Everton, the only team that threatened to break Liverpool's domination of English football during these mid-1980s, knew that they had to win the FA Cup at Wembley one week later, to prevent Liverpool achieving the double. It was a Final which attracted a capacity, 98,000 crowd inside the ground and millions watching the match live on television throughout the world.

The FA Cup Final – Lineker strikes for Everton

Liverpool team-boss Kenny Dalglish made history, as the first player-manager to lead out an FA Cup-Final team at Wembley, when he walked out alongside Everton manager Howard Kendall. While Everton were happy that defender Derek Mountfield had declared himself fit, after injury problems, there was no place in the Liverpool line-up for the luckless Gary Gillespie, victim of a stomach virus on the eve of the Final. So Mark Lawrenson took his place alongside Alan Hansen at the heart of the defence.

Liverpool seemed to settle more quickly, but Everton soon began to get their act together, and inside the first half-hour they had their fans roaring them on as they struck the first blow — Peter Reid put a lofted pass through for Gary Lineker to take in his stride, and he outpaced skipper Hansen. Grobbelaar parried the Everton striker's effort, but Lineker followed up to strike again, and though the Liverpool 'keeper got a second touch to the ball, he couldn't stop it from going into the net. First blood to the Blues.

In the early stages of the second half, Everton pressed for a second goal, and the Liverpool defence appeared to wobble a bit, at times. Twice Grobbelaar had a spot of good fortune, once when Kevin Sheedy rifled a shot across the face of goal, and then Grobbelaar produced an inspired save to tip a goal-bound header from Graeme Sharp over the bar. That save came at a time when Liverpool had just managed to draw level, and it was hailed by many of the onlookers as the turning point of the game.

LEFT: Jan Molby became a cult figure among the Anfield faithful, partly because his refined skill often seemed out of keeping with his thickset frame. His 14 goals were invaluable in bringing the League title to Anfield. RIGHT: Goal-scorer supreme, however, was Ian Rush. With 22 League goals he was top scorer, and in the FA Cup Final he got two. Here he rounds Bobby Mimms for the first.

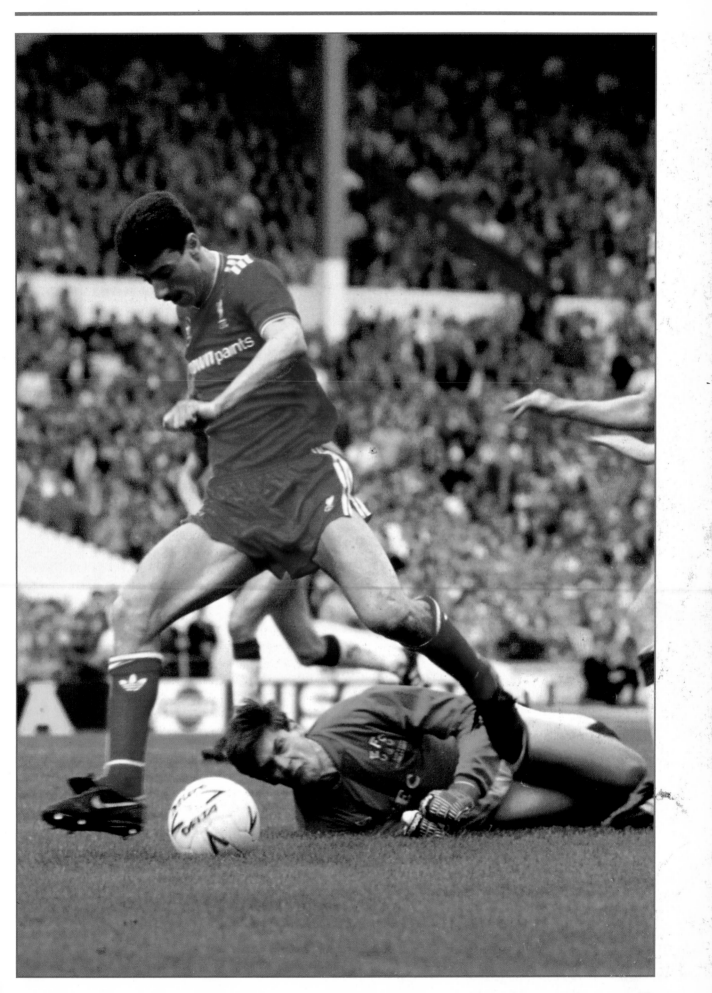

The Liverpool equaliser had arrived via a move which featured Jan Molby and Ian Rush. The Danish international intercepted an Everton clearance and delivered a forward pass which split the Blues' defence. Ian Rush, swift as ever to pounce, took the ball in his stride and advanced on goal. 'Keeper Bobby Mimms came out and did his utmost to block the Liverpool striker, but Rush rounded the 'keeper and drove an angled shot into the net. For the first time, Liverpool had the scent of the double in their nostrils.

Johnston's killer goal, set up by Jan Molby

That goal, and the super-save from Grobbelaar, seemed to send the adrenalin surging through the veins of the men from Anfield, and they began to look like a side convinced of ultimate victory. Once again it was Molby who set up a goal, as he produced a square pass which steered clear of Everton bodies and legs, and as the ball crossed the face of the goal, Craig Johnston was given the time and room to race in and strike from close range to put Liverpool 2-1 ahead.

Everton then tried a new ploy by sending on Adrian Heath, the busy little player who had turned games their way in the past. But this time, there was no way back. When another goal came, it was from Liverpool, and it killed Everton's hopes of a comeback. The ball travelled from Ian Rush to Jan Molby and on to Ronnie Whelan, who crossed precisely for the Welsh international to hammer the ball past Mimms and into the far corner of the net. And that was how the scoreline stayed: Liverpool 3, Everton 1. The dream of a double had finally been turned into reality.

'I don't think that the team quite got the credit that it deserved'

In becoming only the third team this century to achieve this feat, Liverpool had set other records: Kenny Dalglish had become the first player-manager to lead his side to the double. He had also become the first player-manager to collect the Manager-of-the-Year award, and he'd won his 100th cap for Scotland and been made a freeman of the city of his native Glasgow.

Perhaps the most lasting achievement of this remarkable season was the way they had come through some bad spells. Kevin MacDonald, who won a Championship medal that season, believes that the criticism they endured actually helped them, as he explained: 'Early on in the season we were written off by a lot of people after Everton had beaten us. Then we took 34 out of the next 36 points, and we scored a lot of goals. I don't think that the team quite got the credit that it deserved. Ian Rush was prolific that year and Jan Molby had a great season. There was also a tremendous spirit among the team, and the fact that most of the press

had written stories like "End of the Red Machine" only served to spur us on. It really pushed us together to prove what we could do.'

Even though things looked bleak at times, particularly after their defeat by Everton in February, the club remained silent and determined. Alan Hansen remarked on the difference between Liverpool and Manchester United, who started so well but ended up by finishing in fourth place: 'At the start of the season it was said that glory days were returning at Old Trafford. But no boasts should be made until a team has really achieved something. That's the way we have been taught to act at Liverpool and maybe it's something that others should take on board. It may sound like a managerial cliche to "take each game as it comes", but that has been the Liverpool attitude since I joined the club. It was that attitude that saw them win through in the 1985-86 season, even when they weren't playing at their best. Their defeat by Everton, on 22 February, 1986, turned out to be their last of the season.

'Enjoy it, son. This is as good as it gets'

One man who clearly had every confidence in Liverpool's ability to deliver was Phil Neal, who had left Anfield to take charge of team affairs at Bolton Wanderers. In January, 1986, he had declared: 'I've asked Kenny Dalglish to send my Championship medal to Burnden Park when Liverpool win the League title, and I really believe they will do it.' Well, they did.

Everton's manager, Howard Kendall, summed up this season by saying, 'Liverpool had some hiccups early on, but once the team settled down and Kenny Dalglish returned, things began to snowball. Some people may not appreciate just how difficult it is to combine managing and playing — he has done a marvellous job.'

And Kenny Dalglish? This was how he saw it: 'You can never set your stall out to win a specific competition — all you can do is give of your best and hope that your best will be good enough. We gave of our best, and we were rewarded for our efforts with two trophies. So many things can affect results as the weeks go by, but the one constant thing is that you keep on trying to succeed — at least, that's the motto at Liverpool.'

For the double-winning team, there was the satisfaction of becoming the club's greatest achievers, with something no-one could ever take away from them. As Kenny Dalglish said to Craig Johnston after the FA Cup Final victory: 'Enjoy it, son. This is as good as it gets.'

In the 1986 FA Cup Final, Everton played well in the first half and took the lead through Gary Lineker. Jan Molby set up Ian Rush's first goal, the equaliser, with an astute through pass; here, he celebrates Craig Johnston giving Liverpool the lead – and the Dane himself had again been the provider of that vital final ball.

RUNNING THE CLUB

A large part of Liverpool's success can be put down to the administrative side. They have a tradition of getting things right from the Board downwards, and their attitude towards managers and players has been exemplary. The men who run Liverpool are shrewd, tough when they have to be – and utterly dedicated to the club.

Once, a journalist asked John Smith, who joined the Liverpool Board in 1971 and was Chairman of Liverpool from 1973 until he resigned in May 1990 (to be succeeded by Noel White, a Director of the club), why the club was so successful. 'It's because we put our assets out there, on the field,' he replied. People who work at Anfield have a fondness for sayings that capture something special about the atmosphere in which they work. So when you hear a player interviewed after a match saying that the victory was the result of a team effort, he is echoing a statement regularly used by the ex-Chairman himself — 'no-one is bigger than the club.' Over-inflated egos are not tolerated at Anfield. Smith spelt this out when he was asked to assess his own contribution to

Liverpool's success. He was asked if his knowledge of football had helped him in his job as Chairman. 'Never,' he replied. 'We must all know our niche in life. Mine was as an administrator.'

Liverpool-born Smith joined the club as the successful Shankly team of the 1960s was being rebuilt. Smith brought with him an extensive knowledge of business matters — he was a former brewery sales director and also continued as the deputy chairman of an electronics firm — and a proven ability to get the best out of the people he worked with. 'I think I was born to chair meetings,' he said, and sure enough, within two years he was appointed to the post he held until 1990.

Significantly, it was soon after Smith took over that the club decided to abandon its long-established practice of passing the job of Chairman round every three years. The change was instituted very smoothly, without the acrimony that might have accompanied a similar move at another club. This was, in part, testimony to the respect that Smith had already earned, and it certainly turned out well for the club.

Noel White, appointed chairman of Liverpool Football Club in May 1990, in succession to Sir John Smith.

Elections for places on the Board are rarely contested. The records of the Annual General Meetings, where appointments are officially decided, reveal that, as in the recent case of Peter Robinson and the 1971 case of Billy Liddell, people who are nominated simply decline to stand for election if it has been made clear to them that the Board would like another result. Similarly, the 12,000 shares in the club are never quoted on the London stock exchange, and only very occasionally on the Exchange in Liverpool. They are kept in the hands of a comparatively small number of people, whose status is already acknowledged by a network of contacts that have little to do with mere wealth.

It was John Smith who made the decision to keep the team's management in the hands of staff whose abilities were well-known to the club. The often-told story has it that it was Bill Shankly who suggested the

ABOVE: Peter Robinson has served the club since his appointment as club secretary in 1965.

Dalglish when Fagan retired.

It is another indication of the way things are done at Liverpool that jobs are rarely advertised. Even the men and women who work on the turnstiles are replaced by people who are already known to the club. They are often members of the same family. And at Board level, too, people with particular areas of expertise are brought in to meet specific needs when they arise. In 1985, for example, amid all the grief and shame that followed the Heysel tragedy, Smith moved swiftly to recruit the financial and legal expertise that the club was going to need.

Making the right changes at the right time

Almost immediately, it was necessary to show the people of Turin that the club understood their suffering, and Smith made sure that the club co-operated fully with the prosecution of supporters who were responsible for the carnage. It was also necessary, in the interests of the club, to deal with the loss of income that the club would suffer because of the exclusion from European competition. Tony Ensor, the club's solicitor, was promoted to the Board to represent Liverpool's interests in its dealings with UEFA. Noel White, a successful accountant, was recruited in 1987 to assist with the financial challenge resulting from the European ban.

It all adds up to a regime in which everyone knows what is expected of them. This is why when people ask about interference in team matters they are always told that there is none. Of course, the Chairman has a role

John Smith's astute stewardship of the club is one of the major reasons behind its continuing success. His decisions have been shrewd, and he will be missed.

appointment of Bob Paisley to succeed him in 1974. This is not quite true, although it suited everybody at the time that people should think it was. In truth, Bill offered no argument against the choice when he was asked for his opinion. Paisley's replacement, Joe Fagan, was given the job in the face of a great deal of speculation that old boy John Toshack, then Swansea's boss, would be given the job. But Smith favoured Fagan, and it was Smith again who insisted on promoting to play, sometimes a very active one. It was Smith himself who travelled to Sweden to sign Glenn Hysen, who was expected to sign for Manchester United, during the close season of 1989-90. The Chairman's role is all about making sure that the manager has the resources he needs to produce success on the field. For many years, Liverpool has had a policy in its transfer dealings with other clubs that puts the Liverpool manager ahead of the field. Apart from the fact that the club often pays cash for the players it signs, it has operated in the transfer market on the sound business principle that getting the first bid right is at least half the battle in today's cutthroat transfer market. Speed off the mark has often helped Liverpool to secure players coveted by other clubs. The transfer of Dalglish himself, which broke the record for a transfer fee involving British clubs, took, in Smith's words, 'three minutes.'

It is true, of course, that success is much easier to achieve if you are already successful. The task of persuading good players to join the club is made easier by the fact that Liverpool can offer the virtual certainty of winners' medals at the end of the season, and with them very substantial financial rewards. Fifteen employees earned £70,000 and above in the 1988-89 season, with five of them earning well above the £100,000 mark. Win bonuses for a member of the Liverpool squad are also sizeable. In January 1988, the employees package was made even more attractive when Smith announced that the Liverpool pension fund would pay players £100,000 a year at the age of 35. Smith had no worries about the size of the salaries: 'It's such a short working life that I have no qualms about paying them big salaries,' he said.

Starting to think like a big-time club in the Second Division

John Smith would be the first to acknowledge that he is part of a team that includes the people who worked at the club before he arrived. One of his predecessors, TV Williams, had the kind of vision that Smith was later to benefit from. It was Williams who brought Bill Shankly to the club in December 1960. Williams had recognised in the young Scottish manager a fierce ambition and a fanaticism about the game, and he wanted to utilise it for Liverpool's benefit.

Success did not arrive immediately, however. Shankly knew that changes to the playing staff had to be made and he knew who he wanted to buy. He had already attempted to persuade the Huddersfield Board to provide money for two Scottish players he had in mind, but there was resistance from within the board and the deal never got off the ground. It was crucial for the subsequent history of Liverpool, however, that from Williams he was to receive wholehearted support. Williams, acting on a suggestion from John Moores — whose Littlewoods empire straddled most of the parts of Merseyside that were not owned by the Earl of Derby

— appointed Eric Sawyer as the club's Financial Director. Sawyer had gained experience as Managing Director of Littlewoods Foodstores, and this experience was to prove invaluable to Shankly. In a very short time, money was made available for transfers and Ron Yeats and I were signing for what was to become known in the city as Shankly's First Great Team.

'I kept 20,000 tickets under my bed and sold every single one myself'

Peter Robinson was appointed as club Secretary during Sawyer's period as Chairman. Robinson arrived in 1965, after a career in football administration which had taken him to Crewe Alexandra, Scunthorpe United and Brighton and Hove Albion. It was in those early days that Robinson acquired the toughness and realism that were to serve him so well at Anfield. His early days at Crewe were certainly hectic, as he once described: 'When we lost to Spurs in 1960, I kept 20,000 tickets under my bed and sold every single one myself. I used to go home with the money stuffed in every pocket. Crewe had no safe. Now that was a strain. And we lost 13-2. I bought Crewe a safe with the profits.'

Robinson has guided the club through a succession of great teams, each one of which has met the challenge of matching up to the achievements of the one that went before it. He has helped to handle the intense, and sometimes bitter, negotiations over the various contracts that the League has struck with television companies during the 1980s. If Chairman John Smith had most to do with the club's strategic decisions, it is Chief Executive Robinson who has had complete control of implementing them in the day-to-day running of the club's affairs. Robinson chooses the hotel used by the team for its away matches, sits in on transfer discussions and drafts players' contracts. He makes sure that the catering staff prepare everything properly for the benefit of the sponsors, and he handles the press on matters of club policy. In the days of Bob Paisley and Joe Fagan, it was Robinson who tipped off the local journalists about players the club was interested in, usually to make sure that speculation which might damage negotiations was kept to a minimum. And it is through him that the club's finances are organised.

The club's income still comes mainly from its gate receipts. Robinson believes that Liverpool were the last League club that was able to support itself from gate receipts alone. They were also the first in the First Division to negotiate a major sponsorship with a large company (Hitachi). Now, of course, sponsorship accounts for a very large proportion of any successful club's income. But the deals struck with Hitachi, and then Crown Paints, back in the early 1980s came before the decision in 1983 to allow live television cameras into League games. Since then, it has clearly been much easier to sell the space on the club shirts.

Crown Paints provided the club with an income of £500,000 over three years. The deal struck with Japanese electronics firm Candy, in 1988, will be worth even more (over £250,000 a year) now that television plays an even bigger part in the marketing of football. It also helps that Liverpool are the team the public wants to watch. The viewing figures for matches that involve Liverpool are consistently higher — usually about one million viewers — than for matches between other teams. With £145,000 going to the home club for live matches, and £50,000 going to the away club, Liverpool's national popularity earned them £750,000 in the 1989-90 season, once advertising and additional sponsorship have been added to the total.

Low prices, full houses and a fortune from the turnstiles

These are sums that most clubs cannot begin to compete with. Yet most of the club's money — about 70 to 80 per cent — still comes from the people who pay at the turnstiles. The decision made by the Football League in 1983 to allow the home club to keep the whole of the gate money at First Division matches was an important one for all the bigger clubs who could attract attendances of 30,000 and more. It came at an important time for Liverpool. In 1982, after winning yet

Match-day at Anfield, and the paying customers who are the major source of income queue to get in.

The view from ground level at Anfield for the game against Everton in November 1987.

another Championship, the club had to reduce its prices in response to a drop in the average gate from over 40,000 to around 35,000. Since then, ground improvements and rebuilding have reduced capacity, but admission charges are still low and compare favourably with many First and Second Division clubs. The ground's League fixtures were sold out for the whole of the 1988-89 and 1989-90 seasons.

All-seater stadiums and the Taylor Report

Robinson may well have been talking about the enthusiasm and loyalty given to the club by the paying public, when he said: 'From the trading point of view, the income of a football club comes mainly from its turnstiles. So the club really belongs to the supporters.' There is something sentimental about the way even hard-bitten administrators such as Peter view the team's fans. People point to the fact that Liverpool have been reluctant to install the executive boxes, which provide a lucrative source of revenue for many First Division clubs.

But patterns of support are changing, and the club is having to face up to a future which will make sentiment an expensive luxury. Peter Robinson estimates now that around 50 per cent of Liverpool's support at home matches comes from people who live more than 25 miles away from the ground. Well before Lord Justice Taylor had issued his now famous recommendations on terrace standing areas in his report on the Hillsborough tragedy, Liverpool had already made plans for the conversion of the Kop to a seated area. They had realised that they could charge more for a seat and still be able to increase their revenue, even though they would have to reduce their overall ground capacity.

Anfield without the Kop — It's almost unthinkable, isn't it? The massed singing of 'You'll Never

Walk Alone' coming from the comfort of 10,000 seated patrons. The massive redevelopment plans are a good indication of how the administrators of the club have been able to move with the times.

A new Chairman takes over as the new decade begins

For all Peter Robinson's enthusiasm about the club's fans, the people who stand on the Kop don't own the club at all. But the club is owned, organised and managed by people who are just as fanatical in their own way. They are all either lifelong Liverpool supporters, or they arrived late and converted. Provided Liverpool keep on winning they are happy for things to stay as they are. But if staying ahead of the rest requires a reconstruction of the club's finances that necessitates the demolition of the Kop, then the Kop will be demolished.

John Smith, who once chaired a government inquiry into the state of lawn tennis and was awarded the CBE in 1982, has ensured that Liverpool have been one of the most respected institutions in Britain. In May 1990, he stepped down as Chairman to be succeeded by Noel White. Smith, who was knighted in the 1990 New Year's Honours List, said: 'This is the beginning of a new decade for Liverpool Football Club and it is an appropriate time for me to hand over to a younger man. I will continue to serve the club in any capacity.'

The view from behind the goal at Anfield, during the December 1989 game against Manchester United, which ended in a 0-0 draw.

HILLSBOROUGH

The Reds were reaching for the heights again in the 1988-89 season, looking like a good bet to repeat their 'double' triumph of 1985-86. Their semi-final tie in the FA Cup against Nottingham Forest promised a close game between two footballing sides. What actually happened was something out of a nightmare.

Liverpool were due to play Nottingham Forest in an FA Cup semi-final on Saturday 15 April 1989. But now, that date will be remembered not for a football match, but because 95 football fans were crushed to death at the neutral venue, Sheffield Wednesday's Hillsborough ground, in Britain's worst sporting disaster. The tragedy was the city of Liverpool's tragedy., for the dead came from the city, and were typical of its sports fans, with their strong family links to the game. The oldest victim, for example, was 67-year-old Gerard Baron, a retired postal inspector. His brother, Kevin, had worn the red shirt of Liverpool in the 1940s and 1950s, and had won a runners-up medal for Liverpool against Arsenal in the 1950 FA Cup Final.

The crush begins at the Leppings Lane End

At 3.06 p.m. on that fateful Saturday, referee Ray Lewis stopped the FA Cup semi-final between Liverpool and Nottingham Forest at Hillsborough when numerous fans were tumbling over the wire mesh at the Leppings Lane End in a desperate bid to escape the crush that was killing the trapped Liverpool supporters.

Ray Lewis led the players back to their dressing-rooms. One hour and 35 minutes later, they were told the match had been abandoned. While inside the ground thousands had battled to save lives, the players had been in the dressing rooms, unaware of the full scale of the disaster. As Ray Houghton commented: 'We had just sat there waiting and wondering what the hell was going on'

As the full extent of the disaster was becoming clear, Liverpool Football Club braced itself for its biggest challenge: how to help the fans who had so loyally followed them, and who had paid such a fearful price. As Dalglish declared: 'Football is irrelevant when something like this happens.' In the months after, the causes of the disaster would be dissected and analysed, but initially the club's response was a mixture of compassion for the bereaved, and anger that the tragedy had happened at all.

Chairman John Smith, shaking with rage, declared on that afternoon: 'It is an organisational scandal. Why

was Old Trafford not used for this match? They could have split the ground 50-50 there.' There was also anger at the fact that Liverpool supporters had been allocated the Leppings Lane End. As Simon Inglis, author of the *Football Grounds of Great Britain*, noted the day after the disaster: 'The Leppings Lane terrace is less than half the size of the opposite Spion Kop, where Nottingham Forest fans were positioned, yet Liverpool have a much larger average gate and were allocated fewer tickets.'

On that Sunday morning, at the Roman Catholic Metropolitan Cathedral in Liverpool, Bruce Grobbelaar read the first lesson in a memorial service, while Steve Nicol and his wife joined the mourners for a requiem mass. Across the city at Anfield, meanwhile, a more elaborate tribute to the dead was beginning. People were arriving in their thousands to leave flowers. Many were laid at the Bill Shankly Memorial Gates, including a wreath with the message: 'Look after them Shanks. You'll never walk alone'. Many people, however, including John Aldridge, left flowers inside the ground. Club officials took the decision to open the stadium as crowds had built up outside during the morning. Ray Houghton described the scene inside: 'Anfield was a mixture of grief, confusion and calm. Flowers were decorating the Kop goalmouth. A lone voice from the Kop shouted: "Don't worry, we all loved you." And suddenly every one of the players there either burst into tears or held their head in their hands.'

The Kop turned into a garden and a shrine

By 5pm that Sunday, the Kop had become a shrine. During the next week, the rich aroma of freshly-cut flowers filled Anfield as a remarkable pilgrimage of Liverpool fans, numbering about 450,000 in all, came to pay their respects. As Liverpool's groundsman commented: 'It was like walking into an English garden the smell was so sweet.' The saddest Sunday in Liverpool's history ended, for Chief Executive Peter Robinson, with a tele-

In the confusion of the Hillsborough disaster, a fan gestures angrily at Kenny Dalglish.

phone call of sympathy from the president of Juventus Football Club.

On Monday 17 April, Kenny Dalglish and his team went to Sheffield's Royal Hallamshire hospital. Dr David Edbrooke, the consultant anaesthetist, described how Dalglish had spoken to a boy in a coma, and the patient: 'flicked open his eyes and whispered "Kenny Dalglish". It was an amazing recovery.' For the players, the first contact with the victims and their families was extremely painful. As Ray Houghton put it: 'What is there left to feel when a mother asks you to visit her 14-year-old son before she turns off his life-support machine?' On that Monday, 14-year-old Lee Nichol became the 95th fatality of the Hillsborough disaster.

The players attend the funerals of the fans

For the victims' families, the early period was also made particularly painful by the insensitive remarks of the President of UEFA, Jacques Georges. He claimed that the Liverpool fans had displayed 'a frenzy to enter Hillsborough stadium come what may, whatever the risk to the lives of others. One had the impression they were beasts who wanted to charge into an arena. It was not far from hooliganism.' Liverpool were also resisting pressure from the FA about rescheduling the semi-final. On that Monday, Peter Robinson declared: 'We consider it insensitive for the FA to make this request so soon and so placing us under additional pressure at a time of grief. We shall therefore defer consideration of the FA request until next Tuesday.' On Friday 21, players began attending the funerals of the dead fans. Players and their wives were at Anfield to greet bereaved families. As Ronnie Whelan explained: 'Our wives have been magnificent. They have tried so hard to give comfort. It was hard not to share the sorrow of one gentleman who lost his 15-year-old lad. The poor guy couldn't even get a car for the funeral — there are 38 others on the same day.'

On Saturday 22 April, over 500,000 supporters at grounds throughout Britain stood silently for a minute, starting at 3.06, in memory of the dead. At Anfield, in a memorial led by Archbishop Derek Warlock, 15,000 fans inside the ground, and a further 25,000 outside, sang 'You'll Never Walk Alone'.

Liverpool players stood in a long line on the pitch. Steve McMahon stood with John Aldridge, Alan Hansen, Ray Houghton and Craig Johnston, who'd flown back from Australia. For Steve Nicol, there was only one suitable place — on the Kop with the mourners. Former players also came to show their sympathy: Phil Thompson, Sammy Lee from Spain, Terry McDermott, Joe Fagan and John Toshack.

LEFT: The gates at the Leppings Lane End are opened at last and fans are helped away. RIGHT: Police and St John's Ambulance workers aid an elderly man.

Outside, a ribbon of blue and red scarves stretching the full 3/4 of a mile between Anfield and Goodison Park were joined at 3.06. The final link in the chain of scarves — one belonging to 18-year-old Christopher Devenside of Formby Merseyside, who'd died at Hillsborough — was tied by his father, Barry, and Peter Beardsley. Liverpool, meanwhile, had agreed to play Celtic in a friendly at Parkhead to raise money for the Hillsborough Fund.

During this early period the city of Liverpool had been drawn closer to the club. The effect was not lost on Dalglish, who confessed: 'I realised that in all my years as a manager and player, I had miscalculated the importance of the club to the people. It was a mistake. I knew we were important to them, but not how important. It's something I should have realised before.'

The unity of Liverpudlians had also been cemented by the universal contempt for the tabloid press and their treatment of the disaster. One Liverpool fan, who had given his friend mouth-to-mouth resuscitation, said: 'When you give the kiss of life it's like swimming the crawl. You have to come up for air, and as you do so you look down the length of the body towards the legs. Whenever I took a breath in, I saw those photographers clicking away. I couldn't do anything about them. I didn't have the breath.'

Accusations and smears: the press shows its worst side

Further evidence of the tabloids' disgraceful behaviour emerged during the Hillsborough inquiry. Sixteen-year-old Ian Clarke, who gave evidence on crutches, said that in his ward a 'hospital chaplain' speaking to one of the injured turned out to be a journalist: 'It was terrible, they were impersonating doctors, relatives and social workers just to get in. It was most upsetting and they would not give up.' The *Sun*, in particular, earned general condemnation for a story on Wednesday 19 April, headlined 'The Truth', which claimed that Liverpool fans had picked pockets of victims, 'urinated on brave cops' and beaten up PCs giving the kiss of life. The *Sun* report was singled out for criticism by the Press Council as being, 'One-sided, unbalanced and misleading'.

Another common feeling in Liverpool about the Hillsborough disaster was resentment at the police, particularly in the light of their attempts to attribute blame for the disaster to the fans, many of whom, they claimed, were drunk. Indeed, Superintendent David Duckenfield admitted to the Lord Taylor inquiry that he had misled his superiors into believing that the tragedy was caused by Liverpool fans storming the entrance gates. Football fans were being blamed for something that was not at all their fault.

OVERLEAF: Immediate press reaction reflected the overwhelming tragedy. Later press accusations about the behaviour of fans provoked anger in Liverpool.

16 APRIL 1989

No 8,592   Price 60p

ON (APRIL 9) 1,290,000

THE SUNDAY TIMES

Nearly 300 dead or injured in Britain's worst football disaster ● Fans crushed and suffo

Tragedy on the terrace

Afsana Patel 11.5

THE People

FORWARD WITH BRITAIN

35p L

6, 1989 No.5589(P)

SOCCER'S BLOODIEST DISASTER

93 DEAD IN CUP CRUS

...hes vainly for the pulse of a dead fan

28-page

Sunday

33,870

OUR DAY OF TEAR

The toll

93 DEAD, OV

In contrast, the club, its representatives and players had emerged with nothing but credit. As Ray Houghton summed up: 'There is no doubt in my mind that the club have handled the whole situation brilliantly. Liverpool coped with Heysel and now there is Hillsborough. The club will emerge bigger and better for it.'

The official enquiry opens under Lord Justice Taylor

On 16 May, Lord Justice Taylor opened a six-week inquiry into the disaster. Immediately, some of the worst fears about neglect at the stadium were realised. Mr Andrew Collins QC, counsel for the inquiry, questioned the adequacy of the barriers on the Leppings Lane terrace. A newspaper, dated 1931, was discovered stuffed inside one of them.

Elements of the woeful organisation that had contributed to the disaster also came to light. Firstly, a fire brigade computer couldn't find the correct address of the stadium. When fireman had arrived at the ground, there was a terrible lack of communication. As Station Officer John Swain said, 'It would have been as lucky winning the pools to have found a senior police officer able to say what was going on.' Alan Hopkins, Deputy Chief Officer of South Yorkshire Metropolitan Ambulance Service, said that ambulances had to go to the Penistone Road end of the stadium, *opposite* Leppings Lane, as those that went to Leppings Lane could not get in 'because the entrances were too low'.

Lord Justice Taylor's interim report, published on 4 August, attributed much of the blame to the police. Bill Gill, secretary of the Liverpool Supporters Club, said: 'We didn't need a report to tell us that the police were at

ABOVE: The Hillsborough Memorial at Anfield, with the names of all the dead inscribed on it.

fault. Maybe now, however, certain people will admit they were wrong to blame Liverpool supporters.' The report was welcomed by Liverpool Chairman John Smith.

Before the final report was published, though, Liverpool faced another daunting test, when, on 23 November 1989, 228 days after the disaster, Liverpool returned to Hillsborough for a First Division match against Sheffield Wednesday. Steve Nicol commented on the occasion: 'It sounds theatrical to say we were fighting to give people some joy, but that's the way it was. For once, we had the chance to lift them, instead of them lifting us.'

On 29 January 1990, the Home Office published *The Hillsborough Stadium Disaster, Final Report of the*

Inquiry by the Rt Hon Lord Justice Taylor. The 104 page report amounted to a devastating criticism of the state of football. In all, Lord Justice Taylor made 76 recommendations to 'promote better and safer conditions' at stadiums. The major recommendations were: for all-seat accommodation at all sports grounds, with major reductions to commence at the start of the 1990-1991 season; maximum capacity limits for terraces; a review of police operations at grounds; the removal of 'prison type' perimeter fences and a reduction in the height of others to 2.2 metres; and the rejection of the government's proposed National Membership Scheme.

The report was welcomed by Trevor Hicks, whose daughters Victoria, 15, and Sarah, 19, had died in the disaster. He said: 'I'm happy with the report and with

the idea of all-seat grounds. If my daughters had been sitting at Hillsborough, they would still be here today.' The overall conclusion of Justice Taylor, that years of just patching up grounds, enduring periodic disasters and avoiding others by 'muddling through on a wing and a prayer', must be over, was universally accepted.

'Football is a way of life in Liverpool, but it isn't life'

The sadness of Hillsborough will never fade, but for Liverpool Football Club, there had been a graphic realisation of how strong the bond is between the club and those who support it. In his first interview after the disaster, exactly a month after the tragedy, Kenny Dalglish said: 'Not one day has gone by when I haven't thought about it. But it's so much easier for those of us who haven't been bereaved or injured. At the end of the day, they are the ones who are more important that anyone else. And their feelings are more important than anything else.'

One fan who had strong feelings was Barry Devenside, secretary of the Hillsborough Support Group, whose son Christopher had died during the disaster. He summed up his feelings about Hillsborough: 'Football is a way of life in Liverpool, but it isn't life. When you think about what Bill Shankly said about football being more important than life and death, it's ironic that the man who loved football so much from Liverpool made a comment like that. It has come home to roost, hasn't it?'

LEFT: The Kop was transformed into an enormous shrine to those who had died at Hillsborough.

BELOW: Details of the flowers, scarves and banners that festooned the Kop.

...AL
...OROUGH 15TH APRIL 1989

ERIC GEORGE HUGHES	42 YEARS
ALAN JOHNSTON	29 YEARS
CHRISTINE ANNE JONES	27 YEARS
GARY PHILIP JONES	18 YEARS
RICHARD JONES B.Sc	25 YEARS
NICHOLAS PETER JOYNES	27 YEARS
ANTHONY P. KELLY	29 YEARS
MICHAEL KELLY	38 YEARS
CARL DAVID LEWIS	18 YEARS
DAVID WILLIAM MATHER	19 YEARS
BRIAN CHRISTOPHER MATTHEWS	38 YEARS
FRANCIS JOSEPH McALLISTER	27 YEARS
JOHN McBRIEN	18 YEARS
MARIAN HAZEL McCABE	21 YEARS
JOE McCARTHY	21 YEARS
PETER McDONNELL	21 YEARS
ALAN McGLONE "GLONEY"	28 YEARS
KEITH McGRATH	17 YEARS
PAUL BRIAN MURRAY	14 YEARS
LEE NICHOL	14 YEARS
STEPHEN FRANCIS O'NEIL	17 YEARS
JONATHON OWENS	18 YEARS
W. ROY PEMBERTON	23 YEARS
CARL RIMMER	21 YEARS
DAVE RIMMER	38 YEARS
GRAHAM JOHN ROBERTS	24 YEARS
STEVEN ROBINSON	17 YEARS
HENRY CHARLES ROGERS	17 YEARS
ANDREW SEFTON	23 YEARS
INGER SHAH	38 YEARS
PAULA ANN SMITH	26 YEARS
ADAM EDWARD SPEARRITT	14 YEARS
PHILIP JOHN STEELE	15 YEARS
DAVID LEONARD THOMAS	23 YEARS
PAT THOMPSON	35 YEARS
PETER REUBEN THOMPSON	30 YEARS
STUART THOMPSON	17 YEARS
PETER F. TOOTLE	21 YEARS
CHRISTOPHER JAMES TRAYNOR	26 YEARS
MARTIN KEVIN TRAYNOR	16 YEARS
KEVIN TYRRELL	15 YEARS
COLIN WAFER	19 YEARS
IAN "RONNIE" WHELAN	19 YEARS
Mr. MARTIN KENNETH WILD	29 YEARS
KEVIN DANIEL WILLIAMS	15 YEARS
GRAHAM JOHN WRIGHT	17 YEARS

A CITY OF FANS

The supporters of Liverpool Football Club have played no small part in creating the traditions that the club has drawn on. The 'Kop', for example, is the most famous terrace in England, and its wit is legendary. Those who stand on it have had a lot to cheer about – but they themselves have contributed a great deal.

Famed throughout the world, the Kop at Anfield where Liverpool fans have congregated for decades, has an awesome vibrancy and power. During the 1960s, when the Kop was in full voice, I, and every other Liverpool player, felt lifted on to victory when the singing began. And the power of the Kop was certainly not lost on other teams and managers. Back in 1957, Manchester United's boss, Matt Busby, had said: 'That Anfield Spion Kop is one of Liverpool Football Club's prized possessions, and in all seriousness, I am certain that matches have been won through the vocal efforts of its regular patrons.'

Liverpool is a city with the instincts of a family. When times are hard, it closes ranks, weaving a self-protective cocoon around itself, taking on the burden of its grief or hardship; but when the victory is won, it shares its triumph publicly. It is not easy for the outsider to understand this suffering or exuberant show of passion, and often leads to the accusation that Merseysiders carry a large chip on their shoulders, expecting a living from the world, or at least expecting everyone to understand and sympathise with their difficulties. There came a point after Hillsborough when some commentators began to grow weary of the sympathy, never realising nor understanding the impact of the tragedy on the community and the need of the people there for a respectable period of public mourning.

The strength of the Merseyside community

Great Britain was once jokingly said to be made up of England, Ireland, Scotland, Wales and Merseyside. Joke or not, there is more than a grain of truth in it, although Glaswegians would no doubt substitute their own city for Merseyside. And indeed there are remarkable similarities between the two industrial conurbations. Glaswegians, it has to be said, immediately feel at home in the city of Liverpool, none more so than Kenny Dalglish himself. Perhaps it has something to do with the large Irish Catholic populations of both Liverpool and Glasgow where the extended family and the church go hand in hand. The strength of the community stems from the mutual support people have given one another

over years of hardship. Once you begin to understand this, only then do you realise that the city's football teams have become the public face of the city.

Liverpool has always been passionate about its football. A quarter of all the League Championships have come to rest there and it was the first city to boast a *Football Echo*, founded the same year as the Football League (1888). During the 1930s, it created football's first superstar — Dixie Dean — whose fame spread way beyond the boundaries of Britain. For many working class folk, football was the one exciting outlet in their lives. After five and a half days of hard work on the docks, Sunday belonged to the family, but Saturday afternoon belonged to the man. It was cheap, exciting and comradely. You could go alone, you could go with friends but if you wanted to be part of the conversation on Monday morning, you simply had to be part of Saturday afternoon.

Both Liverpool and Everton football clubs have always boasted large followings. Even in the 1950s,

Membership of a religious order is certainly no bar to enjoying a football match, especially when you happen to be a supporter of the best club in the land.

when the two sides were in the doldrums, Goodison could count on the occasional 70,000 crowd while Anfield would attract 60,000. But it was during the 1960s that both clubs took on a new lease of life that would spread beyond the city's borders. At the time, the city was already at the centre of national interest as The Beatles and their music achieved remarkable heights of popularity. This was transferred to the football terraces around the latter part of the 1961-62 season, as Liverpool ran away with the Second Division Championship. The crowds began to chant in unison and clap rhythmically, and as Liverpool clinched the title at Anfield, the supporters refused to leave the ground until their team had reappeared for a lap of honour. Singing on the terraces had been heard at Anfield as far back as 1907, but during this period the activity seemed to become an integral part of the supporters' ritual behaviour.

Songs, chants and chat – the Kop becomes famous

Such was the popularity of the team that anyone hoping to get on to the Kop was obliged to turn up hours beforehand and then suffer a long wait before the game finally got under way. That boredom of waiting, coupled with the incessant playing of Beatles' records over the tannoy, the words of which everyone knew, eventually led to people joining in with them. The television cameras turned up to record it all and the Kop, enjoying its new fame, responded with even more vigour. Success of course bred even greater fervour. New songs were composed, adapted and tried out and as Liverpool won their first FA Cup in 1965, the chant of 'Ee-aye-addio we won der cup' rang around Wembley to the amusement of the watching nation.

At the heart of the relationship between Liverpool Football Club and the city is the Kop, emblem of fanaticism and colour. It was built in 1906, and named Spion Kop after a hill in South Africa where a Merseyside regiment had suffered heavy losses during the Boer War. More than 300 had died, many of them local Liverpool lads in pursuit of the strategically important hilltop. A journalist on the Liverpool Echo hit on the novel idea of naming the cinder banking after the hilltop. In 1928, it was extended and roofed so that 30,000 could watch from its terraces. It is still an imposing sight and anyone climbing its steps for the first time cannot help but be impressed when they reach the top and look down at the terracing tumbling beneath them towards the goalmouth. Today, its capacity has been severely reduced and it will soon change dramatically once the terracing and crash barriers have been torn down and replaced with seats. But when it was filled to capacity with

Liverpool fans urge their team on at the 1989 FA Cup Final against Everton at Wembley, a contest the Reds won 3-2.

30,000 spectators in the 1960s and 1970s, it was an awe-inspiring sight that brought both a combination of fear and elation to visiting teams. And above all, the sound that boomed and echoed from within its roof was, as Bill Shankly used to say, worth at least a goal start. When Inter Milan visited Anfield in 1965 for a European Cup semi-final and came on to the pitch making for the Kop end, they were forced to turn tail and race in the opposite direction, such was the clamour of noise that greeted them.

Serving an apprenticeship on the Kop

Uncomfortable though the Kop may be, you cannot call yourself a true Liverpool supporter until you have served your apprenticeship on its sweaty, noisome terraces. It was not unusual on those great European nights to find yourself at half time some 20 yards or more from where you had been at kick off. It was certainly dangerous and in retrospect it was a wonder there was never a serious accident. Youngsters beginning their support of Liverpool always make for the Kop. Here they serve their time, moving to the stands as they get older, and perhaps a little richer. But beneath its massive canopy, the bellowing within the Kop is what draws them. 'At times I swear I could visibly see the Kop sucking the ball into the net,' Bill Shankly once remarked.

When Liverpool go a goal down they are traditionally at their most dangerous as the Kop resounds with a new roar, its pride somehow hurt by an opposition that dares to score against them. So often dull games have suddenly been transformed by an opposition goal, and Liverpool is spurred into action as the Kop reawakens and the volume is turned up. It is rare, though not unknown, for the Anfield crowd to criticise its own. As long as a player is part of the family, he will be supported; only when he leaves the family might feelings of resentment be vented.

The Kop and Kevin Keegan - from favourite son to outcast

Kevin Keegan was once a hero of the Kop, but when he deserted Anfield at the height of his career for new challenges on the Continent, the Kop responded like a family whose brother has walked out. Rightly or wrongly, it was regarded as an act akin to treachery, and the esteem with which he had been regarded disappeared almost overnight. Only weeks before, he had helped Liverpool to the European Cup, but his love affair with the club was now over and the recriminations soon began. When Keegan returned to Anfield with his new side, Hamburg, in the European Super Cup six months later, they were trounced 6-0, with the Kop vocally mocking Keegan's decision to move abroad. Keegan has rarely returned to Anfield and is now almost a forgotten name in the annals of the club.

The Kop's favourites: Ronnie Rosenthal becomes an overnight hero

Contrast that with Graeme Souness, whose similar decision to move abroad after he had loyally given the best years of his playing career to Liverpool, was acknowledged. He has remained a friend and at the end of last season, as he sat in the stands, the Kop spotted him and chanted his name, affectionately remembering the delight he had brought during his Anfield days. Souness is still part of the family. Others like Jimmy Case and Sammy Lee who left Anfield are still highly regarded, although this also has much to do with the fact that they were born in the city.

The Kop of course has its favourites, none more so than Kenny Dalglish, who has been their hero as player and now as manager. Yet it can also welcome new players with open arms as it has Ronnie Rosenthal, who overnight became an instant hero. For many years, Emlyn Hughes, or 'Crazy Horse' as he was known, was a firm favourite. Hughes, the outsider, soon struck a rapport with the crowd, and was welcomed into the shelter of the family. But others such as Nigel Spackman and Michael Robinson never quite caught the imagination and their departures brought few tears.

David Johnson's transfer. Did the Kop affect the outcome?

David Johnson was another who owed much to the Anfield crowd. With the signing of Dalglish and the presence of Toshack in the side, Johnson looked to be on the verge of leaving as the 1977-78 season kicked off. He had already asked for a transfer and had been left out of the side for the Charity Shield game against Manchester United. As he walked towards the Liverpool crowd, gathered over Wembley's tunnel during that game, Johnson received an enthusiastic welcome. It was a magnanimous gesture by the Koppites, especially for one who appeared to be on the verge of leaving. But within the week, Johnson had changed his mind, was back off the transfer list and was fighting for his place in the team. The crowd's attitude may not have been the deciding factor, but they certainly let Johnson know that his presence at Anfield was valued. Although he made few appearances that season, Johnson eventually linked up with Dalglish to share a formidable partnership as he struck 18 goals the next season and 27 the following. His goalscoring form earned him an international call-up.

If the Kop favours its own, it can be equally generous to the opposition. Visiting goalkeepers delight in taking the applause as they run towards the Kop goal. Liverpool have a long history of good goalkeepers and Anfield crowds recognise goalkeeping talent when they see it. Record-breaker Peter Shilton always collects the loudest cheer. And when Pat Jennings once saved two penalties in front of the Kop, their groans were immediately followed by applause for the great Irishman. They can also be scathing, as when Gary Sprake of Leeds United foolishly hurled the ball into his own net, an act that was fittingly followed by a chorus of 'Careless Hands'. On every successive visit, Sprake was reminded of his mistake. And even Peter Shilton has been reminded more than once of his nocturnal misdemeanours. But the Kop can be magnanimous. When Arsenal scored in the final thrilling minute, to clinch the League Championship at Anfield in May 1989, it was the Kop who stood and applauded their triumph, recognising that their own team had been fairly and squarely beaten.

A single voice suggests a line, and thousands take it up

The wit of the Kop is famous. Ask Derby County's giant 6ft 7in midfielder Kevin Francis who was subjected to a chorus of 'There's only one Blackpool Tower' when he came on as substitute last season. Nobody seems sure where the chants and humour originate — the pundits have puzzled over it for years. But from somewhere deep down in the depths of the Kop, a single voice will suggest a line and within seconds, thousands will have joined in. Perhaps this is part of the attraction of standing in the Kop — trying to initiate a chant of your own, and becoming a cheerleader.

Unlike other major football clubs, Liverpool have retained their homely links. They employ just a handful of officials, the club is run on a tight budget and is usually deserted except on match days. It is perhaps because Liverpool have clung on to their tradition of 'keeping it in the family' that they have managed to retain their links with the local community. When unemployment was high in the city during the 1980s, there was a deliberate policy to keep prices down and even now at £135 for the best season ticket, prices are among the lowest in the First Division. There are no super-rich executive boxes, no powerful families running the club's affairs and nobody is allowed to think that they are more important than the club itself. It may well be that Liverpool undersells itself but this may not necessarily be a bad thing in these days of over-commercialisation.

Anfield's surroundings are still very much those traditionally associated with a northern English football club. The stadium rises majestically between rows of terraced houses, barely a couple of miles and a cheap bus ride away from the city centre. From the late 1980s, though,

1986 – 'double' year – and Liverpool fans have a right to celebrate and enjoy the sensation of being part of the 'Anfield machine'.

things were changing in the ground. The vast majority of spaces available, including on the Kop itself, have become reserved for ticket holders, making it very difficult to plan the occasional or casual visit. Three sides of the ground have become fully seated — and this has the effect of further highlighting the vociferous nature of the Kop.

The arrival of John Barnes and the Kop's dilemma

The Koppites have had to adjust to more than just changing physical surroundings. Their well-known racism, for example, was called into question when John Barnes was regularly receiving their loudest cheers. As Rogan Taylor, who helped found the Football Supporters' Association, said: 'When Everton fans abused John Barnes, it solidified Barnes in their affection, because somebody they had taken to their hearts was being treated in the same way they'd treated black players for years. I'm quite sure that if Everton had bought Barnes, the situation would have been mirrored because the potential for that behaviour existed at both

The legendary 'Kop', famous for its wit and undying support, but also for its knowledge and its generosity, especially to opposing goalkeepers (who often have the opportunity to shine at Anfield).

clubs. So Barnes has had a tremendous impact in making people realise that once you've accepted a black player you can't go hooting another one. It's been interesting watching the Kop go through the transformation, realising that it's impolite to John to boo someone else who's black.'

Rival managers often complain about playing at Anfield — arguing that Liverpool's crowd intimidates and earns them an unjust amount of penalties. In 1988, Manchester United's manager, Alex Ferguson, said: 'I can understand why clubs go from here biting their tongues and choking on their own vomit, knowing they've been done by referees. In this intimidating atmosphere, you need a miracle to win.' Indeed, Terry Venables, the Tottenham manager went even further, declaring: 'The Anfield crowd is different from what it was 10 years ago. When we played them [in November 1989] there was a nastiness about them that disappointed me.'

The reputation of Liverpool's fans was severely tarnished by the incidents at the Heysel Stadium in 1985. Previously, they had been among the most well-behaved and welcome visitors to Europe, and their celebrations in Rome after the European Cup win of 1977 were treated with amusement rather than horror by the Italians. Heysel ended all that.

Support for the club stretches far from Merseyside

Yet whatever their critics may feel, Liverpool fans are secure in the knowledge that they have a sense of place and identity that London fans, for example, rarely experience. And support for the club now stretches way beyond the boundaries of Merseyside. Each week coachloads pour in from the Midlands, Scotland and London, while a couple of planes fly in from Dublin and Belfast. Liverpool's support is changing. At the centre there is still the Liverpudlian football fanatic, but on the fringes a variety of regional accents and even foreign languages can be detected. And there are more women than ever supporting the club. But the wit and humour

will remain. To stand on the Kop, scarf held aloft, singing 'You'll Never Walk Alone', is to be part of the family that is Liverpool Football Club.

The River Mersey and the derelict waterfront of a city that has been in the economic doldrums while it has enjoyed the highest level of sporting success.

A NEW TEAM AND NEW TRIUMPHS

After the double triumph, Liverpool comprehensively rebuilt their team, and created a side that played some of the most expansive attacking football the English game had yet seen. They ended the decade even more dominant a force than they had been ten years earlier.

Cup and League doubles are rare, but in his first season as player-manager, Kenny Dalglish had managed what Bill Shankly, Joe Fagan and Bob Paisley had failed to achieve: The League and FA Cup 'double'. In the process, Dalglish became only the third manager this century to achieve the feat. This remarkable success, however, did not deflect Dalglish from restructuring the team in an attempt to produce a team capable of repeating that triumph.

Kenny Dalglish's first signing was the former Everton midfield star Steve McMahon, in September 1985. He was bought from Aston Villa for £350,000. Although he has not been able to emulate the sheer authority of Graeme Souness as the midfield linchpin of the Liverpool team, McMahon has given the midfield great power, as the Arsenal manager George Graham explained: 'McMahon is one of the best midfield players in Britain. He is a great all-round tackler and passer and has excellent shooting ability.' It is surprising, in fact, that McMahon has not scored more goals for the club.

Dalglish was to make many further changes, especially in the season after the double. In 1986-87, Dalglish drafted in Barry Venison from Sunderland and Nigel Spackman from Chelsea. But they were not fundamental signings and Liverpool did not have a brilliant season by their standards. They went out of the FA Cup in the third round, losing 3-0 to Luton Town on the plastic pitch at Kenilworth Road, and the one real chance of a trophy vanished when they were beaten at Wembley by Arsenal in the Littlewoods Cup Final.

Liverpool took only one point from their last four away games in the League, and the Championship went to Howard Kendall's Everton. This 'failure' was the cue for significant reconstruction by Dalglish. Ian Rush left for Juventus after six seasons and 207 first team goals. There had been a year's warning of Rush's departure, but it was going to be difficult to replace a player who

had become virtually synonymous with Liverpool's success. But Liverpool had started to blood his replacement, John Aldridge, who had been signed from Oxford United in January 1987 for £750,000, and was initiated into the 'Liverpool way' in the reserves during the latter part of that season.

'My forte was looking for crosses in the box and getting on the end of them'

In Liverpool's opening League game of the 1987-88 season, which was away to Arsenal, Aldridge, and the two other major pre-season signings — John Barnes and Peter Beardsley — made their mark immediately. In the match against Arsenal at Highbury, Aldridge scored in Liverpool's 2-1 victory. In an excellent start to his Anfield career, John Aldridge scored 11 goals in his first 10 games. Aldridge had a superb three years at the club, scoring 50 League goals in 83 League appearances. Once again, Liverpool had shown that they were experts in the transfer market.

Aldridge himself was aware of the difficulties for new players learning the Liverpool way: 'When Kenny bought me in January 1987,' he said, 'my initial period at Liverpool was tricky. I found it difficult adjusting to their style of play, because of the emphasis on through balls. That was the style they had used with Ian Rush. But it began really working for me at Liverpool only when they bought John Barnes and Ray Houghton, because that was my forte, looking for crosses into the box and getting on to the end of them. Once they came into the team it was certainly easier. But Kenny knew that was my game when he bought me. And he used me that way

John Barnes – as exciting a player as Liverpool have ever had, and in the flying left-wing tradition of Billy Liddell, Peter Thompson and Steve Heighway.

for Liverpool. Liverpool know how to get the best out of players. I think that the reason Liverpool are so successful is that they keep things simple. Players have said it before, but that is the explanation. They keep it basic and simple. "Don't try and do anything extraordinary or difficult. Just play the easy ball." That's what the message from Ronnie Moran and Roy Evans is all the time: "Play and move, play and move!"'

'...the finest exhibition I've seen the whole time I've watched the game'

And this dynamic new attacking trio of Aldridge, John Barnes and Peter Beardsley, could not have had a better season. Liverpool were playing at their glorious best and they equalled Leeds United's record under Don Revie of 29 League games without defeat. Liverpool's run was ended at Goodison Park by Everton, who won with a solitary goal by Wayne Clarke.

In 1988, Liverpool came close to equalling their achievement of 1986. After defeating Nottingham Forest 2-1 at Hillsborough on 9 April 1988 in the FA Cup semi-final, they met Brian Clough's team at Anfield in the League four days later. Liverpool, with goals from Aldridge (two), Houghton, Gillespie and Beardsley, won 5-0 and produced one of the best performances of the decade. The former Preston North End forward Tom Finney, who won 76 caps for England and scored 249 goals in 569 first class performances, was among many who praised the Liverpool performance that night. Finney said: 'It was the finest exhibition I've seen the whole time I've played and watched the game. It was absolutely tremendous. You couldn't see it bettered anywhere. Not in Brazil even. Not at that pace. The moves they put together were fantastic.'

John Aldridge's Cup Final penalty – and Dave Beasant's save

Liverpool rolled inexorably on in the League and at Anfield, on 23 April, Peter Beardsley sealed their 17th Championship in a 1-0 win against Spurs. But the double evaded them again when they were beaten 1-0 by unfancied Wimbledon in the FA Cup Final. To add to Liverpool's disappointment, John Aldridge, the First Division's leading scorer that season, and a master penalty taker, watched in agony as Dave Beasant became the first goalkeeper ever to save a penalty at Wembley in an FA Cup Final. Aldridge's spot kick had cost them the double once again. Not for the last time in the latter 1980s, were Liverpool, when they should have waltzed through weaker opponents, unable to raise their game.

LEFT: Gary Gillespie has often been troubled by injury, but this classy Scots defender is also a scorer of goals, and here troubles the Arsenal defence.

Liverpool had performed admirably in winning the League, but as the new season approached, this meant little to the management. When, in July 1988, the Liverpool players were being handed their Championship medals, Ronnie Moran warned them: 'Last season meant nothing. Get yourself in shape to do it all again!'

The double was lost again in 1988-89, but this time the final failure did not come at Wembley. After enduring the trauma of the Hillsborough disaster, and all the subsequent wranglings about whether the FA Cup would actually continue that season, Liverpool came through to defeat Everton at Wembley. They won 3-2, after extra time, with goals from Aldridge and two superb extra time goals from their substitute Ian Rush, who had rejoined the club in August 1988. Because of Hillsborough, Kenny Dalglish commented, this match had meant more than any other victory: 'Sometimes you have to wait for the satisfaction to sink in,' he said, 'but this was immediate and emotional.'

Sweden's captain Glenn Hysen was snatched from under Manchester United's nose in the summer of 1989, partly to cover Alan Hansen and partly to add quality to the defence as a whole.

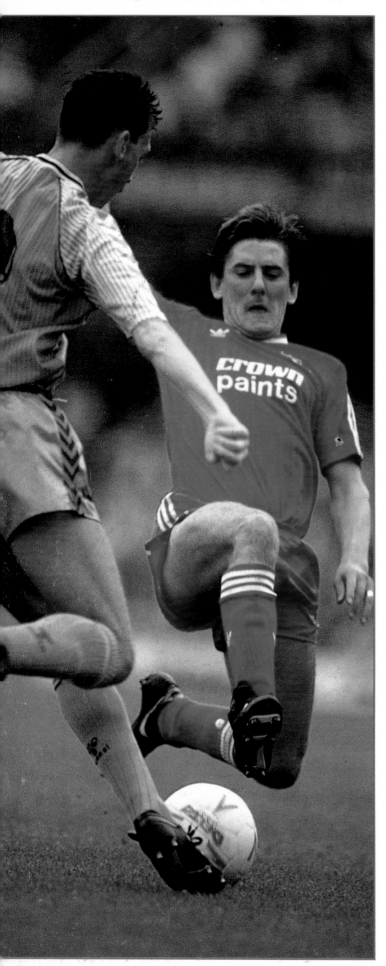

Winning the League seemed to be a mere formality. A 5-1 drubbing of relegation-bound West Ham on 23 May left them needing only to avoid defeat by Arsenal by two clear goals to retain the title. Better still for Liverpool, Arsenal, who had to come to Anfield needing to win, had lost on their seven previous visits to Anfield. But on the night, George Graham's side possessed the stronger will to win. As Graham himself said: 'Liverpool did not really entertain the possibility of defeat. Because they knew that losing 1-0 would be enough, they weren't as positive as us.' Graham's men were more determined and although there was some dispute about Alan Smith's goal, there could be no arguments about Michael Thomas's superb last-gasp winner which ended Liverpool's run of 24 games without defeat. However, the new champions were warmly, and sportingly, applauded by the Kop.

There was speculation in the weeks after the defeat, that the result would mark a significant turning point in British soccer. In short, many predicted that the era of Liverpool domination was at an end. But the foundations of that success were too firmly laid for one defeat to shatter them. Indeed, despite this remarkable victory by Arsenal, Liverpool's side of 1988-89 had been as consistent as ever: only six defeats in 38 games.

'There are no stars there...you get treated like everyone else at Anfield'

Liverpool's method of playing has remained the core of the success and it has remained the club's greatest asset. The Liverpool style in the late 1980s was a rare combination of technique, skill and effort. But all the great players of the 1980s — from Souness to Barnes — learned that no matter how good they were, the success of the individual was nothing compared to the success of the team. Anyone big-headed was brought immediately, and harshly, back down to size.

As former captain Phil Neal said: 'Liverpool are a team on the pitch and off. There are no stars there. It doesn't matter if you cost £30,000, £300,000 or are worth £3 million, you get treated like everyone else at Anfield. Ian Rush, for example, is the first to say that his success owes a lot to the graft of others. He knows and appreciates that for him to be the striker he is — and he is brilliant — that he needs worker bees.'

In the last three seasons, there have been three key worker bees. In 1988-89, Ronnie Whelan missed only one League game, and Ray Houghton and Steve Nicol were ever-presents. Whelan joined the club in October

LEFT and RIGHT: Peter Beardsley gets in a tackle against Coventry during the match of August 1987 that Liverpool won 4-1. Beardsley himself had a tremendous season that year. With his tricky running and accurate short passes he proved an excellent foil to Barnes and Aldridge.

1979 from the Dublin amateur club Home Farm (their manager was an Anfield scout), and scored on his debut against Stoke at Anfield on 3 April 1981, at the age of 19. He was a regular by 20, bringing zest and pace to the left wing.

As the years passed, Whelan has adapted and matured his game. As George Graham explained: 'I think one of the reasons that the Liverpool team of the late 1980s was so dynamic, was they had John Barnes playing a great wide role, superb in one-on-one situations, but, just as important, they had Ronnie Whelan backing him up. He plays such an unselfish but critical role, winning the ball and then supplying it well.'

The enigma – producing the goods for Liverpool but not in internationals

Steve Nicol, honoured by the Professional Footballers' Association as their Player of the Year in 1989, is one of Liverpool's soundest players, able to fulfil a role for them in many departments. As Kenny Dalglish said: 'It's one thing to be able to play in three or four positions, but another to play well in all of them. Steve is a great credit to the club.'

But Nicol, like his England colleague Barnes, has had trouble repeating his excellent club form at international level. Scotland's manager, Andy Roxburgh, believes that Nicol has trouble adjusting to the fact that with Scotland he does not get the all-round support that he does when he's with Liverpool. As he explained: 'I have to own up over Steve Nicol and agree that he's an enigma. I think I know several reasons why he changes, but so far it hasn't helped me to correct it. There seems to be little doubt that he has a "security" problem, inasmuch as leaving Anfield and the nourishment he gets there is like leaving the womb. He has trouble being comfortable with himself.'

Republic of Ireland international Ray Houghton, who was such a vital part of Jack Charlton's World Cup quarter-finalists, was one of Liverpool's best signings of the 1980s. His ceaseless running and general contribution to the midfield have been vital in allowing John Barnes to adopt the free attacking role that has brought the team such reward. His vital contribution has not been lost on Mark Lawrenson, who commented: 'Ray has a great engine, he's very effective and always works very hard. For Liverpool he reminds me very much of Ian Callaghan. He can keep the ball, he can get it back when it's lost and he inspires other players.'

Perhaps Kenny Dalglish's most spectacular transfer success has been John Barnes. When Dalglish bought Barnes, he was acquiring a phenomenally skilful player, but one whom Dalglish believed would be refined and improved at Anfield. Dalglish believed that for all his individual brilliance, Barnes would extend his game immeasurably by fitting into Liverpool's traditional passing game. Significantly, Dalglish also realised that Barnes's superb winger's skills — his dribbling,

crossing and shooting ability — would add a potent dimension to Liverpool's play.

Dalglish was also unconcerned about upsetting any bigots: 'The signing of Barnes is something I've never regretted. I know that he was good enough. I certainly had no qualms about signing him because of his colour. It didn't even cross my mind.' And so Barnes became the first black player to sign for Liverpool. Barnes, who has topped the First Division scoring chart in 1990, and who was awarded the Professional Footballers' Association Player of the Year award in 1988, and the Football Writers' Association Player of the Year award in 1988 and 1990, has been a glorious success for Liverpool.

Former England manager Bobby Robson, who first selected the young Barnes for England in May 1983, is one of many in the game who has been particularly struck by how a great player is able to make even greater progress by being 'schooled' at Anfield. As Robson explained: 'When Liverpool paid Watford £900,000 for Barnes, they were obviously buying a hugely talented player. But Watford's style wasn't really helping John. He was still good enough to show what he could do, but once he arrived at Liverpool, there was suddenly a real difference, because John was playing with other top class players. At Liverpool, the service he gets — really accurate balls to feet in positions where he can deal with it comfortably and turn the situation immediately into a dangerous one — has made such a terrific difference to his game. He doesn't have to fight for the ball at Liverpool, he gets it right to his feet. He has become a truly world class player while he's been at Anfield.'

'...we knew that they were good enough to fit in with what we want'

So in Whelan, Nicol, Aldridge, Houghton and Barnes, Liverpool bought players with vastly different styles who were at different stages in their careers, harnessed their unique skills and blended them into a superb unit. As Bob Paisley commented: 'Liverpool aren't overridden with tactics. The first thing that is drilled into new players is that they should play their own game. We've bought them because we knew that they were good enough to fit in with what we want.'

In Kenny Dalglish, the Liverpool Board have the perfect Anfield manager. He is loyal to the Liverpool methods of management, but more importantly, he has shown himself in his transfer dealings to be well able to maintain the winning system. He has remained true to the Anfield philosophy of putting the team first. As he so succinctly put it in 1988: 'The people who come to watch us play, who love the team and regard it as part of their lives, would never appreciate Liverpool having a huge balance in the bank. They want every asset we possess to be wearing a red shirt, and that's what I want, too.'

Barry Venison slotted in quietly and efficiently at full-back after joining the club from Sunderland. His strengths have been in his soundness and reliability.

Liverpool can afford to buy the best — the team that lost the title decider to Arsenal (ironically, a largely homegrown team) had cost just under £10 million — but during the 1980s they produced little from their own nurseries. The Anfield youth set up is rigorous and exacting, but not very fruitful. There have been precious few successes. In the 1988-89 season, Gary Ablett and Steve Staunton, who both established themselves in the first team, were the first players to come through from the junior ranks since Sammy Lee in 1980. During the entire successful decade, Ablett and Staunton were two of only six players who Liverpool used that they had developed in their own youth team.

'Any boy who makes it to the first team at Anfield is special'

Malcolm Cook, formerly Liverpool's Youth Development Officer, who left the club in the summer of 1988 to go into teaching, remarked of Staunton's achievement at progressing through from the Anfield ranks: 'Any boy who makes it to the first team at Anfield is special. The odds are heavily stacked against them, and they seemed stacked against Steve when he arrived.' Staunton, who was signed from Dundalk in August 1986, impressed Cook greatly. As Cook said: 'Steve captained our youth squad at a tournament in Eindhoven in 1987 and his game went up a dimension. I was very proud of him. I tried to get him to set himself the target of getting in the first team.'

Although this was a great challenge, Staunton was up to it. He later commented: 'The great plus at Anfield is that with so many great players around you, you tend to grow up quickly when you get into the team. The down side is that competition for places is so keen that you are never sure of staying in it. On balance, I'll settle for the first.'

But even when youngsters get into the first team at Anfield they are not allowed to let their heads be turned.

OVERLEAF: Ian Rush had some difficulty in slotting back into the side after his return from Italy in the 1988-89 season, perhaps because he was missing the service he used to get from Kenny Dalglish. But in the FA Cup Final of 1989 against Everton, he slipped into top gear when he came on as substitute. TOP LEFT: Rush finds a vital bit of space and turns to shoot past Kevin Ratcliffe. TOP RIGHT: Neville Southall vainly attempts to parry the ball. BOTTOM LEFT: Rush's second and decisive goal of the match – he slides in to steer the ball into the corner, and is already getting to his feet (BOTTOM RIGHT) as it crosses the line past Southall. CENTRE: Rush wheels away in triumph after his first goal.

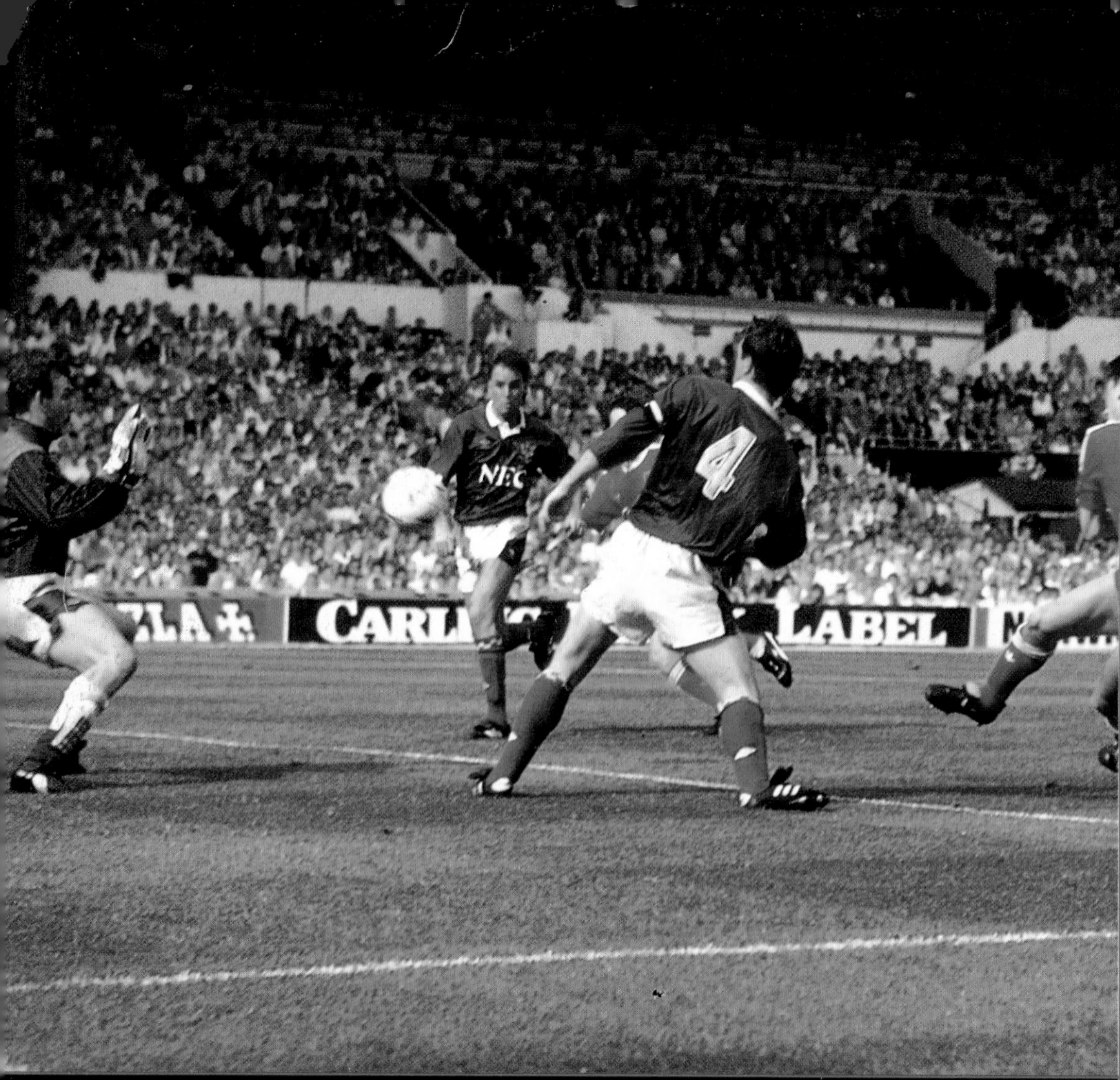
LABEL
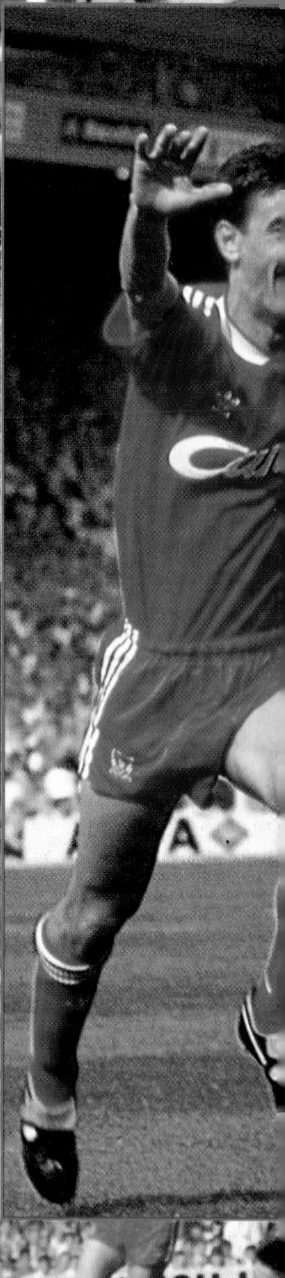
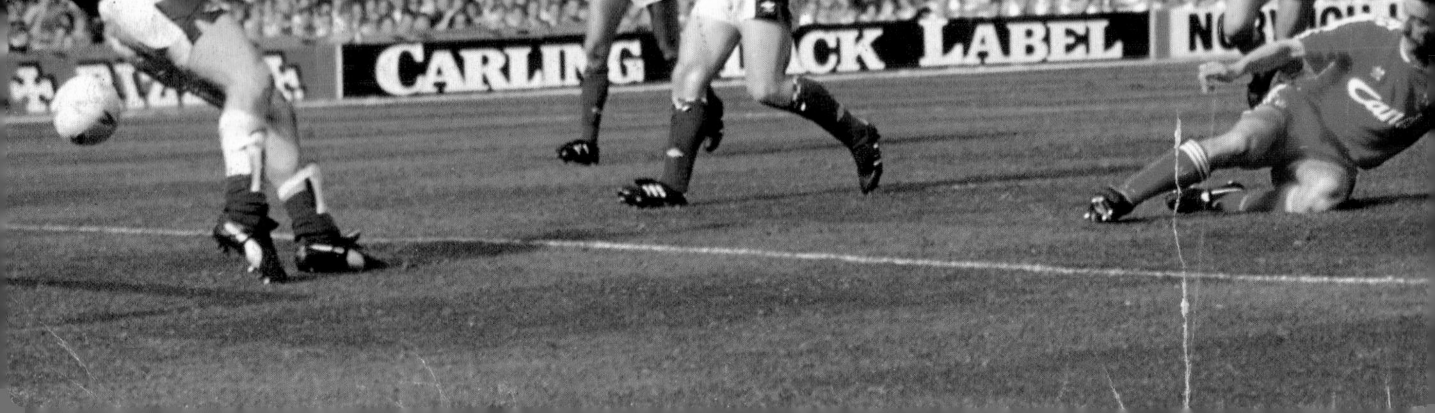
CARLING
LABEL

When Staunton made his debut for the Republic of Ireland in October 1988 at the age of 19, just weeks after making his first-team debut for Liverpool as a substitute in the home game against Spurs — he still did not have his own pair of boots. Maurice Setters, Jack Charlton's assistant, recalled: 'I had to go round with the president of the Football Association of Ireland to try and get him a pair. I said to the lad, "Won't Kenny Dalglish buy you some?" But Liverpool are like that. They make these young players earn their corn.'

'Every time I receive the ball there are five or six options open to me'

Staunton and Ablett may point to a slight change at Anfield. As Malcolm Cook said just before leaving Anfield: 'We have 16-year-old boys pushing for a place in the reserves and this would not have happened in the past.' If Liverpool can supplement their brilliant transfer dealings with a steady flow of talent from their own youth system, it will make them all the stronger.

During the last two seasons, Dalglish's transfer dealings have been relatively limited. At the start of the 1989-90 season he bought 19-year-old Steve Harkness from Carlisle United and transferred Kevin MacDonald to Coventry and Jim Beglin to Leeds. More importantly, he also bought Sweden's captain, Glenn Hysen, from Fiorentina for £650,000. Hysen was immediately impressed by Liverpool's training methods: 'Training sessions at Melwood are very tough, but you have only

to see the end result to know it is successful. Fitting into the team has been a dream; it's so easy. Every time I receive the ball there are five or six options open to me. I thought Gothenburg were pretty good when we won the UEFA Cup. Milan, Juventus and Napoli are all high class — but I would back this Liverpool team, without hesitation, against any European side.'

Although the new Liverpool — with John Barnes and Ian Rush forming a deadly attacking duo supported by Beardsley and with Houghton, Whelan and McMahon pushing through from midfield — is an extremely exciting unit, Alan Hansen, when asked to sum up the best Liverpool team of his time, said: 'I'd have to give it to the team of 1978 and 1979, which had Ray Clemence, Phil Thompson, Terry McDermott, Graeme Souness and Kenny Dalglish at their peak. As soon as I'd got the ball I looked for Kenny. You could hit it five or six yards either side of him and it didn't matter, his control was so good and he was so strong. It was a hell of a side. It was more of a team, less individualistic than the team of 1989-90, but it still played some brilliant football.'

Throughout the 1980s, Liverpool forged resilient teams and the team in 1989-90 needed this special strength of character. Although the 1989-90 team may have been a less consistent team than some of the earlier Championship-winning sides, they did produce

Moments to go in the final match of the 1988-89 season, and Arsenal's Michael Thomas just squeezes the ball past Grobbelaar and Nicol.

Thomas celebrates his goal, as Nicol and Grobbelaar turn in disbelief, realising that the 'double' is beyond them in these final seconds of the 1989 Arsenal game.

some outstanding performances, full of imaginative attacking. Perhaps the finest was in September 1989, when Liverpool thrashed Steve Coppell's Crystal Palace 9-0 at Anfield. It was a game in which John Aldridge, playing his last game for Liverpool before his £1 million move to Real Sociedad, scored with a penalty. At the end, Aldridge joyfully hurled his boots into the Kop.

Revenge in the FA Cup semi-final for Crystal Palace

The stunning win equalled the club's record victory margin, with eight different players getting their names on the score-sheet — a record for the First Division. Kenny Dalglish's team returned to the top of the First Division with a display that evoked all the finesse and power of the 'classic' 5-0 drubbing of Nottingham Forest 18 months before, but which possessed more consistency of purpose and four more goals. That 9-0 victory and their 6-1 win at Coventry, were the highest home and away victories in the Division that season. Less consistent the new team may have been, but they were maestros when going forward.

After that defeat, Crystal Palace's manager Steve Coppell said: 'I think this will haunt us for the rest of our lives. I didn't feel humiliated at the end — just

completely numb like my players. They came into the dressing room as though they had just gone 15 rounds with a heavyweight.' It is ironical that it was Palace who showed up Liverpool's inconsistency in April 1990, when they beat Liverpool 4-3 in the FA Cup semi-final at Villa Park. Liverpool, who had played as though they were on a different plain to Crystal Palace on that Anfield night in September 1989, were beaten, just seven months later, by the same team. Liverpool were again by far the better team, but at Villa Park Palace exposed Liverpool's weakness at defending against set pieces. And as Alan Hansen commented: 'We were so far in control that we relaxed and allowed Palace back into the game.'

'It's a question of working even harder and believing in what we do'

Liverpool continued to play well in the League and did eventually win through. It had been a season when they had overcome some (by their standards!) average spells. During one particularly poor period before Christmas they really struggled. When they were beaten 3-2 by Queen's Park Rangers in November 1989, they had suffered their fourth defeat in five matches. But the players were convinced they would get it right. John Barnes said at the time: 'We have all talked about what is happening. But nothing will change. It will come right in the end. It's a question of working even harder and believing in what we do. There is no other way. Remember, we are only sticking to the same style that has been so successful, so why change now?' Kenny Dalglish was more precise, warning that only total effort would do. Those players who did not give this complete level of commitment were, he warned, 'no use to us or themselves.' Such is the fierce competition for places at Anfield, and the quality of players who have to struggle even to get on to the substitute's bench, that Peter Beardsley, once Britain's most expensive player, spent much of 1989-90 fighting for a first-team place.

Although many commentators were predicting that Liverpool had worn themselves out — and that Graham Taylor's Aston Villa were going to snatch the League Championship — Liverpool grew in strength as the season reached its end. Indeed, Dalglish even had a very potent card up his sleeve to play right at the death: the Israeli international Ronnie Rosenthal. Introduced in April, he revived Liverpool's attack, scoring a hat-trick on his full League debut away to Charlton Athletic in April 1990, when Peter Beardsley was dropped. Rosenthal, who was signed on loan from Standard Liege in Belgium, scored seven goals for Liverpool in five matches and ensured that his 'on loan' status would change: on 27 June 1990, Dalglish signed him for £1 million on a three-year contract.

When Liverpool won their 18th title on 28 April, by beating Queen's Park Rangers 2-1 at Anfield, they had once again proven their doubters wrong. Although Hansen

was to lead the players in a cheerful champagne-imbued chorus of 'We're forever blowing doubles', a wry reflection on the remarkable number of times that the team had come so close to making history, he responded to the criticism that had been levelled at the team after their shock FA Cup defeat by saying: 'People have been criticising us since we were beaten in the semi-final by Crystal Palace, but we have lost only one League game in the 22 we've played since last November. That is Championship form and it speaks for itself.'

'Nothing has changd in ten years – only the faces'

So Liverpool had won their 18th title and their 31st trophy in the last 20 years. The 1980s had been as brilliant as the 1970s, and the club could approach the 1990s with optimism. Former midfield star Jimmy Case, now at Southampton, said after playing against Liverpool in 1990: 'Nothing has changed in 10 years. Only the faces.' The constant flow of fresh talent into the team, always successfully blooded into the Liverpool way, will ensure continued triumphs at Anfield. There is little doubt that before the 1990-91 season is finished, whether Liverpool have retained their title or not, Kenny Dalglish will have started on a new rebuilding programme for the team, to guarantee that success

continues. One thing is certain, every new player will have instilled into him Dalglish's philosophy, which was described by Alan Hansen: 'This club has enjoyed success for the last 20 years and will for the next 20. The manager has a saying: "A for attitude and C for commitment." If we remember that, no team in the country can beat us.'

Alan Hansen is quite aware that Liverpool's continued success will not be left to chance. Although Dalglish's interventions in the transfer market in 1989 were relatively modest, during the season there were a host of potential purchases that were being closely monitored. Liverpool know, above all else, that it is the quality of players that is decisive. As Alan Hansen, the only player to have spanned the whole of the 1980s, said: 'It is the players that win Championships. The back room staff do their bit and the manager buys the best players. Once the players are on the field it is up to them. Everyone knows that we have the best players.'

But those players will not be allowed to rest on their reputations or their past achievements. At Liverpool, they must be continually rebuilding the temple. As former captain Phil Neal, who shares with Hansen the record of eight League Championship medals, said: 'I can tell you that at Liverpool you soon get it drummed into you that the last year is worth nothing.' The club will never accept second best. That is the motto that Anfield will take into the 1990s.

LEFT: The 'secret weapon' of the 1990 run-in to the title was undoubtedly Ronnie Rosenthal, whose speed and lethal finishing blitzed all the defences he came up against.

Celebrations for the Championship in 1990 between (from left) Rosenthal, Rush, Whelan, Hansen and Barnes. But can Liverpool match their achievments of the 1980s in the new decade?

THE STATISTICS

Liverpool's record season by season, from 1979/80 to 1989/90, inclusive, including details of Liverpool scorers and all the players who turned out for the first team

During the 11 seasons under review, Liverpool played 631 matches, winning 368 (58.32 per cent), losing 108 (17.11 pe cent) and drawing 155 (24.56 per cent).

They scored 1,210 goals (1.91 per match) and conceded 523 (0.82 per match).

During this period they won the League Championship seven times, were second three times and fifth once. They won the League Cup four times, the European Cup twice and the FA Cup twice, were losing finalists in three competitions and losing semi-finalists in five.

1979/80

Played 59 Won 34 Lost 10 Drawn 15 Goals for 107 Goals against 41

Appearances (including appearances as substitute): Neal, Dalglish, Thompson 59, Clemence, Souness 58, R Kennedy 55, Johnson 53, Hansen, McDermott 52, Case 51, A. Kennedy 50, Fairclough 27, Heighway, Lee 11, Irwin 10, Cohen 5, Ogrizovic 1.

Goals: Johnson 28, Dalglish 20, McDermott, Fairclough 13, R Kennedy 9, own goals 7, Case 5, Hansen 4, Irwin, Souness 2, Cohen, A Kennedy, Neal, Thompson 1.

Total home attendance (27 matches): 1,182,674. Average 43,803.

August
21 D1 Bolton H 0-0
25 D1 West Brom H 3-1 Johnson 2, Owen og
28 LC Tranmere A 0-0

September
 1 D1 Southampton A 2-3 Johnson, Irwin
 4 LC Tranmere H 4-0 Thompson, Dalglish 2, Fairclough
 8 D1 Coventry H 4-0 Johnson 3, Case
15 D1 Leeds A 1-1 McDermott
19 EC Dinamo Tbilisi H 2-1 Johnson, Case
22 D1 Norwich H 0-0
25 LC Chesterfield H 3-1 Fairclough, Dalglish, McDermott
29 D1 N Forest A 0-1

October
 3 EC Dinamo Tbilisi A 0-3
 6 D1 Bristol C. H 4-0 Johnson, Dalglish, R Kennedy, McDermott

 9 D1 Bolton A 1-1 Dalglish
13 D1 Ipswich A 2-1 Hunter og, Johnson
20 D1 Everton H 2-2 Lyons og, R Kennedy
27 D1 Manchester C. A 4-0 Johnson, Dalglish 2, R Kennedy
30 LC Exeter H 2-0 Fairclough 2

November
 3 D1 Wolves H 3-0 Dalglish 2, R Kennedy
10 D1 Brighton A 4-1 R Kennedy, Dalglish 2, Johnson
17 D1 Spurs H 2-1 McDermott 2
24 D1 Arsenal A 0-0

December
 1 D1 Middlesbrough H 4-0 McDermott, Hansen, Johnson, R Kennedy
 5 LC Norwich A 3-1 Johnson 2, Dalglish
 8 D1 Aston V. A 3-1 R Kennedy, Hansen, McDermott
15 D1 C Palace H 3-0 Case, Dalglish, McDermott
22 D1 Derby A 3-1 Davies og, McDermott, Johnson
26 D1 Man United H 2-0 Hansen, Johnson
29 D1 West Brom A 2-0 Johnson 2

January
 5 FA Grimsby H 5-0 Souness, Johnson 3, Case
12 D1 Southampton H 1-1 McDermott
19 D1 Coventry A 0-1
22 LCSF N Forest A 0-1
26 FA N Forest H 2-0 Dalglish, McDermott

February
 9 D1 Norwich A 5-3 Fairclough 3, Dalglish, Case
12 LCSF N Forest H 1-1 Fairclough
16 FA Bury H 2-0 Fairclough 2

D1 – League match. **FA** – FA Cup. **LC** – League Cup, later Milk Cup and then Littlewoods Cup. **EC** – European Cup. **ES** – European Super Cup. **WC** – World Champions Cup. **SF** – Semi-final. **F** – Final. **A** – Away match. **H** – Home match. **N** – Neutral ground.

19 D1 N Forest H 2-0 McDermott, R Kennedy
23 D1 Ipswich H 1-1 Fairclough
26 D1 Wolves A 0-1

March
 1 D1 Everton A 2-1 Johnson, Neal
 8 FA Spurs A 1-0 McDermott
11 D1 Man City H 2-0 Caton og, Souness
15 D1 Bristol C. A 3-1 R Kennedy, Dalglish 2
19 D1 Leeds H 3-0 Johnson 2, A Kennedy
22 D1 Brighton H 1-0 Hansen
29 D1 Spurs A 0-2

April
 1 D1 Stoke H 1-0 Dalglish
 5 D1 Man United A 1-2 Dalglish
 8 D1 Derby H 3-0 Irwin, Johnson, Osgood og
12 FASF Arsenal N 0-0
16 FASF Arsenal N 1-1 Fairclough
19 D1 Arsenal H 1-1 Dalglish
23 D1 Stoke A 2-0 Johnson, Fairclough
26 D1 C Palace A 0-0
28 FASF Arsenal N 1-1 Dalglish

May
 1 FASF Arsenal N 0-1
 3 D1 Aston V. H 4-1 Johnson 2, Cohen, Blake og
 6 D1 Middlesbrough A 0-1

1980/81

Played 62 Won 30 Lost 10 Drawn 22 Goals for 112 Goals against 57
Appearances: Neal 62, Clemence, R. Kennedy 61, McDermott 59, Lee 55, Souness 54, Dalglish, Hansen 53, Johnson 40, Thompson 39, Case 35, A. Kennedy 33, Irwin 26, Cohen 18, Fairclough, Money 16, Heighway 10, Rush 9, Gayle 5, Ogrizovic, Russell, Sheedy, Whelan 1.
Goals: McDermott 21, Dalglish 18, Johnson, R. Kennedy, Souness 13, Lee 9, Fairclough 7, own goals 5, A Kennedy 4, Neal 3, Hansen 2, Case, Gale, Irwin, Whelan 1.
Total home attendances (31 matches) 1,167,020. Average 37,645.

August
16 D1 C Palace H 3-0 Dalglish, R Kennedy , A Kennedy
19 D1 Coventry A 0-0
23 D1 Leicester A 0-2
27 LC Bradford C. A 0-1
30 D1 Norwich H 4-1 Hansen, McDermott, A Kennedy, Johnson

September
 2 LC Bradford C H 4-0 Dalglish 2, R Kennedy, Chapman og
 6 D1 Birmingham A 1-1 Dalglish
13 D1 West Brom H 4-0 McDermott, Souness, Fairclough 2

17 EC Oulun Palloseura A 1-1 McDermott
20 D1 Southampton A 2-2 Souness, Fairclough
23 LC Swindon H 5-0 Lee 2, Dalglish, Cockerill og, Fairclough
27 D1 Brighton H 4-1 Souness 2, Fairclough, McDermott

October
 1 EC Oulun Palloseura H 10-1 Souness 3, McDermott 3 Fairclough 2, Lee, R. Kennedy
 4 D1 Man City A 3-0 Dalglish, Souness, Lee
 7 D1 Middlesbrough H 4-2 McDermott 2, R Kennedy, Dalglish
11 D1 Ipswich H 1-1 McDermott
18 D1 Everton A 2-2 Lee, Dalglish
22 EC Aberdeen A 1-0 McDermott
25 D1 Arsenal H 1-1 Souness
28 LC Portsmouth H 4-1 Dalglish, Johnson 2, Souness

November
 1 D1 Stoke A 2-2 Johnson, Dalglish
 5 EC Aberdeen H 4-0 Miller og, Neal, Dalglish, Hansen
 8 D1 Forest H 0-0
11 D1 Coventry H 2-1 Johnson 2
15 D1 C Palace A 2-2 R Kennedy, McDermott
22 D1 Aston V H 2-1 Dalglish 2
25 D1 Wolves A 1-4 Neal
29 D1 Sunderland A 4-2 Johnson, McDermott, Lee 2

December
 2 LC Birmingham H 3-1 Dalglish, McDermott, Johnson
 6 D1 Spurs H 2-1 Johnson, R Kennedy
13 D1 Ipswich A 1-1 Lee
20 D1 Wolves H 1-0 R Kennedy
26 D1 Man United A 0-0
27 D1 Leeds H 0-0

January
 3 FA Altrincham H 4-1 McDermott Dalglish 2, R Kennedy
10 D1 Aston V A 0-2
14 LCSF Man City A 1-0 R Kennedy
17 D1 Norwich A 1-0 McDermott
24 FA Everton A 1-2 Case
31 D1 Leicester H 1-2 Young og

February
 7 D1 West Brom A 0-2
10 LCSF Man City H 1-1 Dalglish
14 D1 Birmingham H 2-2 Johnson, Neal
21 D1 Brighton A 2-2 Johnson, McDermott
28 D1 Southampton H 2-0 R Kennedy, McDermott

March
 4 EC CSKA Sofia H 5-1 Souness 3, Lee, McDermott
14 LCF West Ham N 1-1 A Kennedy
18 EC CSKA Sofia A 1-0 Johnson
21 D1 Everton H 1-0 Bailey og
28 D1 Arsenal A 0-1

April
 1 LCF West Ham N 2-1 Dalglish, Hansen
 3 D1 Stoke H 3-0 Whelan, McDermott 2

8 ECSF Bayern Munich H 0-0
11 D1 N Forest A 0-0
14 D1 Man United H 0-1
18 D1 Leeds A 0-0
22 ECSF Bayern Munich A 1-1 R Kennedy (won on away goal)
25 D1 Spurs A 1-1 Gayle

May
 2 D1 Sunderland H 0-1
 5 D1 Middlesbrough A 2-1 R Kennedy, Irwin
19 D1 Man City H 1-0 R Kennedy
27 ECF Real Madrid N 1-0 A Kennedy

1981/82

Played 62 Won 39 Lost 10 Drawn 13 Goals for 129 Goals against 46
Appearances: Grobbelaar, Neal 62, Dalglish 61, Lawrenson 60, Souness 54, Hansen 53, Lee, Rush 49, McDermott, Thompson 48, A. Kennedy, Whelan 47, Johnson 25, R. Kennedy, Johnston 23, Sheedy 4.
Goals: Rush 30, Dalglish 22, McDermott 20, Whelan 14, Johnson, Johnston 7, Souness 6, Lawrenson, Lee 4, A Kennedy, R Kennedy, Neal 3, Hansen, own goals, Sheedy 2.
Total home attendances (29 matches) 931,499. Average 32,120

August
29 D1 Wolves A 0-1
September
 1 D1 Middlesbrough H 1-1 Neal
 5 D1 Arsenal H 2-0 McDermott, Johnson
12 D1 Ipswich A 0-2
16 EC Oulun Palloseura A 1-0 Dalglish
19 D1 Aston V H 0-0
22 D1 Coventry A 2-1 A. Kennedy, McDermott
26 D1 West Ham A 1-1 Johnson
30 EC Oulun Palloseura H 7-0 Dalglish, McDermott 2,
R. Kennedy, Johnson, Rush, Lawrenson

October
 3 D1 Swansea H 2-2 McDermott 2
 7 LC Exeter H 5-0 Rush 2, McDermott, Dalglish, Whelan
10 D1 Leeds H 3-0 Rush 2, Cherry og
17 D1 Brighton A 3-3 Dalglish, R. Kennedy, McDermott
21 EC AZ Alkmaar A 2-2 Johnson, Lee
24 D1 Man United H 1-2 McDermott
28 LC Exeter A 6-0 Rush 2, Dalglish, Neal, Sheedy, Marker og
31 D1 Sunderland A 2-0 Souness, McDermott

November
 4 EC AZ Alkmaar H 3-2 McDermott, Rush, Hansen
 7 D1 Everton H 3-1 Dalglish 2, Rush .

11 LC Middlesbrough H 4-1 Sheedy, Rush, Johnson 2
21 D1 West Brom A 1-1 Dalglish
28 D1 Southampton H 0-1

December
 1 LC Arsenal A 0-0
 5 D1 N Forest A 2-0 Lawrenson, R Kennedy
 8 LC Arsenal H 3-0 Johnston, McDermott, Dalglish
13 WC Flamengo N 0-3
24 D1 Manchester C H 1-3 Whelan

January
 2 FA Swansea A 4-0 Hansen, Rush 2, Lawrenson
 5 D1 West Ham H 3-0 McDermott, Whelan, Dalglish
12 LC Barnsley H 0-0
16 D1 Wolves H 2-1 Whelan, Dalglish
19 LC Barnsley A 3-1 Souness, Johnson, Dalglish
23 FA Sunderland A 3-0 Dalglish 2, Rush
26 D1 Notts Co. A 4-0 Whelan, Rush 3
30 D1 Aston V A 3-0 Rush, McDermott 2

February
 2 LCSF Ipswich A 2-0 McDermott, Rush
 6 D1 Ipswich H 4-0 McDermott, Rush, Dalglish, Whelan
 9 LCSF Ipswich H 2-2 Rush, Dalglish
13 FA Chelsea A 0-2
16 D1 Swansea A 0-2
20 D1 Coventry H 4-0 Souness, Lee, Rush, McDermott
27 D1 Leeds A 2-0 Souness, Rush

March
 3 EC CSKA Sofia H 1-0 Whelan
 6 D1 Brighton H 0-1
 9 D1 Stoke A 5-1 McDermott, Dalglish, Souness, Lee, Whelan
13 LCF Spurs N 3-1 Whelan 2, Rush
17 EC CSKA Sofia A 0-2
20 D1 Sunderland H 1-0 Rush
27 D1 Everton A 3-1 Whelan, Souness, Johnston
30 D1 Birmingham H 3-1 Rush 2, McDermott

April
 2 D1 Notts Co. H 1-0 Dalglish
 7 D1 Man United A 1-0 Johnston
10 D1 Man City A 5-0 Lee, Neal, Johnston, A Kennedy, Rush
13 D1 Stoke H 2-0 A Kennedy, Johnston
17 D1 West Brom H 1-0 Dalglish
24 D1 Southampton A 3-2 Rush, Whelan 2

May
 1 D1 N Forest H 2-0 Johnston 2
 3 D1 Spurs A 2-2 Dalglish 2
 8 D1 Birmingham A 1-0 Rush
11 D1 Arsenal A 1-1 Rush
15 D1 Spurs H 3-1 Lawrenson, Dalglish, Whelan
18 D1 Middlesbrough A 0-0

D1 – League match.   **FA** – FA Cup.   **LC** – League Cup, later Milk Cup and then Littlewoods Cup.   **EC** – European Cup.   **ES** – European Super Cup.   **WC** – World Champions Cup.   **SF** – Semi-final.   **F** – Final.   **A** – Away match.   **H** – Home match.   **N** – Neutral ground.

1982/83

Played 59 Won 37 Lost 12 Drawn 10 Goals for 119 Goals against 50

Appearances: Grobbelaar, Neal 59, Souness 58, Dalglish, A Kennedy, Lee 57, Lawrenson 54, Hansen 51, Rush 50, Johnston 46, Whelan 40, Hodgson 36, Thompson 33, Fairclough 11, Nicol 4, McDermott 3.

Scorers: Rush 30, Dalglish 20, Neal, Souness 11, Johnston 10, Hodgson 9, Lawrenson, Whelan 7, A Kennedy 6, Fairclough 4, Lee 3, own goal 1.

Total home attendance (31 matches) 993,104. Average 32,036.

August
28 D1 West Brom H 2-0 Lee, Neal
31 D1 Birmingham A 0-0

September
 4 D1 Arsenal A 2-0 Hodgson, Neal
 7 D1 N. Forest H 4-3 Hodgson 2, Souness, Rush
11 D1 Luton H 3-3 Souness, Rush, Johnston
14 EC Dundalk A 4-1 Whelan 2, Rush, Hodgson
18 D1 Swansea A 3-0 Rush 2, Johnston
25 D1 Southampton H 5-0 Whelan 2, Souness, Lawrenson 2
28 EC Dundalk H 1-0 Whelan

October
 2 D1 Ipswich A 0-1
 5 LC Ipswich A 2-1 Rush 2
 9 D1 West Ham A 1-3 Souness
16 D1 Man United H 0-0
19 EC JK Helsinki A 0-1
23 D1 Stoke A 1-1 Lawrenson
26 LC Ipswich H 2-0 Whelan, Lawrenson
30 D1 Brighton H 3-1 Lawrenson, Dalglish 2

November
 2 EC JK Helsinki H 5-0 Dalglish, Johnston, A Kennedy 2, Neal
 6 D1 Everton A 5-0 Rush 4, Lawrenson
10 LC Rotherham H 1-0 Johnston
13 D1 Coventry H 4-0 Dalglish, Rush 3
20 D1 Notts Co A 2-1 Johnston, Dalglish
27 D1 Spurs H 3-0 Neal, Dalglish 2
30 LC Norwich H 2-0 Lawrenson, Fairclough

December
 4 D1 Norwich A 0-1
11 D1 Watford H 3-0 Rush, Neal 2
18 D1 Aston V A 4-2 Hodgson, Dalglish, A Kennedy, Rush
27 D1 Man City H 5-2 Dalglish 3, Neal, Rush
28 D1 Sunderland A 0-0

January
 1 D1 Notts Co. H 5-1 Dalglish 2, Rush 3
 3 D1 Arsenal H 3-1 Rush, Souness, Dalglish
 8 FA Blackburn A 2-1 Hodgson, Rush,
15 D1 West Brom A 1-0 Rush
18 LC West Ham H 2-1 Hodgson, Souness
22 D1 Birmingham H 1-0 Neal
29 FA Stoke H 2-0 Dalglish, Rush

Febuary
 5 D1 Luton A 3-1 Rush, A Kennedy, Souness
 8 LCSF Burnley H 3-0 Souness Neal Hodgson
12 D1 Ipswich H 1-0 Dalglish
15 LCSF Burnley A 0-1
20 FA Brighton H 1-2 Johnston
26 D1 Man United A 1-1 Dalglish

March
 2 EC Widzew Lodz A 0-2
 5 D1 Stoke H 5-1 Dalglish 2, Neal, Johnston, Souness
12 D1 West Ham H 3-0 Pike og, Lee, Rush
16 EC Widzew Lodz H 3-2 Neal, Rush, Hodgson
19 D1 Everton H 0-0
22 D1 Brighton A 2-2 Rush 2
26 LCF Man United N 2-1 A Kennedy, Whelan

April
 2 D1 Sunderland H 1-0 Souness
 4 D1 Man City A 4-0 Fairclough 2, Souness, A Kennedy
 9 D1 Swansea H 3-0 Rush, Lee, Fairclough
12 D1 Coventry A 0-0
16 D1 Southampton A 2-3 Dalglish, Johnston
23 D1 Norwich A 0-2
30 D1 Spurs A 0-2

May
 2 D1 N. Forest A 0-1
 7 D1 Aston V. H 1-1 Johnston
14 D1 Watford A 1-2 Johnston

1983/84

Played 66 Won 37 Lost 13 Drawn 16 Goals for 118 Goals against 45.

Appearances: Grobbelaar, Hansen, A. Kennedy 66, Lawrenson 65, Rush 64, Neal 63, Souness 60, Lee 57, Johnston 51, Dalglish 50, Robinson 39, Nicol 37, Whelan 34, Wark 9, Hodgson 7.

Goals: Rush 47, Dalglish, Robinson, Souness 12, Whelan 9, Nicol 7, Johnston 4, Lee, Neal, own goals 3, A Kennedy 2, Wark 2, Hansen, Hodgson 1.

Total home attendance (31 matches) 937,175. Average 30,231.

August
27 D1 Wolves A 1-1 Rush
31 D1 Norwich A 1-0 Souness

September
 3 D1 N Forest H 1-0 Rush
 6 D1 Southampton H 1-1 Rush
10 D1 Arsenal A 2-0 Johnston, Dalglish
14 EC Odense A 1-0 Dalglish
17 D1 Aston V. H 2-1 Dalglish, Rush

24 D1 Man United A 0-1
21 EC Odense H 5-0 Dalglish 2, Clausen og, Robinson 2

October
 1 D1 Sunderland H 0-1
 5 LC Brentford A 4-1 Rush 2, Robinson, Souness
15 D1 West Ham A 3-1 Robinson 3
19 EC Atletico Bilbao H 0-0
22 D1 QPR A 1-0 Nicol
25 LC Brentford H 4-0 Souness, Hodgson, Dalglish, Robinson
29 D1 Luton H 6-0 Rush 5, Dalglish

November
 2 EC Atletico Bilbao A 1-0 Rush
 6 D1 Everton H 3-0 Rush, Robinson, Nicol
 8 LC Fulham A 1-1 Rush
12 D1 Spurs A 2-2 Robinson, Rush
19 D1 Stoke H 1-0 Rush
22 LC Fulham H 1-1 Dalglish
26 D1 Ipswich A 1-1 Dalglish
29 LC Fulham A 1-0 Souness

December
 3 D1 Birmingham H 1-0 Rush
10 D1 Coventry A 0-4
17 D1 Notts Co. H 5-0 Nicol, Souness 2, Hunt og, Rush
20 LC Birmingham A 1-1 Souness
22 LC Birmingham H 3-0 Nicol, Rush 2
26 D1 West Brom A 2-1 Nicol, Souness
27 D1 Leicester H 2-2 Lee, Rush
31 D1 N. Forest A 1-0 Rush

January
 2 D1 Man United H 1-1 Johnston
 6 FA Newcastle H 4-0 Robinson, Rush 2, Johnston
14 D1 Wolves H 0-1
17 LC Sheffield Wed. A 2-2 Nicol, Neal
20 D1 Aston V A 3-1 Rush 3
24 LC Sheffield Wed. H 3-0 Rush 2, Robinson
29 FA Brighton A 0-2

February
 1 D1 Watford H 3-0 Rush, Nicol, Whelan
 4 D1 Sunderland A 0-0
 7 LCSF Walsall H 2-2 Whelan 2
11 D1 Arsenal H 2-1 A Kennedy, Neal
14 LCSF Walsall A 2-0 Rush, Whelan
18 D1 Luton A 0-0
25 D1 QPR H 2-0 Rush, Robinson

March
 3 D1 Everton A 1-1 Rush
 7 EC Benfica H 1-0 Rush
10 D1 Spurs H 3-1 Dalglish, Whelan, Lee
16 D1 Southampton A 0-2

21 EC Benfica A 4-1 Whelan 2, Johnston, Rush
25 LCF Everton N 0-0
28 LCF Everton N 1-0 Souness
31 D1 Watford A 2-0 Wark, Rush

April
 7 D1 West Ham H 6-0 Rush 2, Whelan, Dalglish, Souness 2
11 ECSF Dinamo Bucharest H 1-0 Lee
14 D1 Stoke A 0-2
18 D1 Leicester A 3-3 Whelan, Rush, Wark
21 D1 West Brom H 3-0 McNaught og, Souness, Dalglish
25 ECSF Dinamo Bucharest A 2-1 Rush 2
28 D1 Ipswich H 2-2 A Kennedy, Rush

May
 5 D1 Birmingham A 0-0
 7 D1 Coventry H 5-0 Rush 4, Hansen
12 D1 Notts Co. A 0-0
15 D1 Norwich H 1-1 Rush
30 ECF Roma N 1-1 Neal (won 4-2 on penalties)

1984/85

Played 63 Won 33 Drawn 15 Lost 15 Goals for 107 Goals against 49
Appearances: Grobbelaar, Hansen, Neal 63, Wark 61, Whelan 58, Dalglish 52, Lawrenson 49, A. Kennedy 48, Nicol 47, Rush 42, Walsh 39, MacDonald 25, Lee, Molby, Gillespie 24, Johnston 17, Beglin 15, Robinson 10.
Scorers: Wark 27, Rush 26, Walsh 13, Whelan 12, Nicol 7, Dalglish 6, Neal 5, own goals 2, Beglin, Lawrenson 2, Gillespie, A. Kennedy, Molby, Robinson 1.
Total attendances (29 matches) 996,273. Average 34,354.

August
25 D1 Norwich A 3-3 Bruce og, Dalglish, Neal
27 D1 West Ham H 3-0 Walsh, Wark 2

September
 1 D1 QPR H 1-1 Whelan
 4 D1 Luton A 2-1 Neal, Dalglish
 8 D1 Arsenal A 1-3 A Kennedy
15 D1 Sunderland H 1-1 Walsh
19 EC Lech Poznan A 1-0 Wark
22 D1 Man United A 1-1 Walsh
24 LC Stockport A 0-0
29 D1 Sheffield Wed H 0-2

October
 3 EC Lech Poznan H 4-0 Wark 3, Walsh
 6 D1 West Brom H 0-0
 9 LC Stockport H 2-0 Robinson, Whelan
12 D1 Spurs A 0-1

D1 – League match.   **FA** – FA Cup.   **LC** – League Cup, later Milk Cup and then Littlewoods Cup.   **EC** – European Cup.   **ES** – European Super Cup.   **WC** – World Champions Cup.   **SF** – Semi-final.   **F** – Final.   **A** – Away match.   **H** – Home match.   **N** – Neutral ground.

20 D1 Everton H 0-1
24 EC Benfica H 3-1 Rush 3
28 D1 N Forest A 2-0 Whelan, Rush
31 LC Spurs A 0-1

November
3 D1 Stoke A 1-0 Whelan
7 EC Benfica A 0-1
10 D1 Southampton H 1-1 Rush
18 D1 Newcastle A 2-0 Nicol, Wark
24 D1 Ipswich H 2-0 Wark 2

December
1 D1 Chelsea A 1-3 Molby
4 D1 Coventry H 3-1 Wark 2, Rush
9 WC Independiente N 0-1
15 D1 Aston V A 0-0
21 D1 QPR A 2-0 Rush, Wark
26 D1 Leicester H 1-2 Neal
29 D1 Luton H 1-0 Wark

January
2 D1 Watford A 1-1 Rush
5 FA Aston V H 3-0 Rush 2, Wark
16 ES Juventus A 0-2
19 D1 Norwich H 4-0 Wark, Rush 2, Dalglish
27 FA Spurs H 1-0 Rush

February
2 D1 Sheffield Wed A 1-1 Lawrenson
12 D1 Arsenal A 3-0 Rush, Neal, Whelan
16 FA York A 1-1 Rush
20 FA York H 7-0 Wark 3, Whelan 2, Neal, Walsh
23 D1 Stoke H 2-0 Nicol, Dalglish

March
2 D1 N. Forest H 1-0 Wark
6 EC FK Austria A 1-1 Nicol
9 FA Barnsley A 4-0 Rush 3, Whelan
16 D1 Spurs H 0-1
20 EC FK Austria H 4-1 Wark 2, Nicol, Obermayer og
23 D1 West Brom H 5-0 Nicol, Dalglish, Wark 3
31 D1 Man United H 0-1

April
3 D1 Sunderland A 3-0 Rush 2, Wark
6 D1 Leicester A 1-0 Whelan
10 ECSF Panathinaikos H 4-0 Wark, Rush 2, Beglin
13 FASF Man United N 2-2 Whelan, Walsh
17 FASF Man United N 0-1
20 D1 Newcastle H 3-1 Wark, Gillespie, Walsh
24 ECSF Panathinaikos A 1-0 Lawrenson
27 D1 Ipswich A 0-0

May
3 D1 Chelsea H 4-3 Whelan, Nicol 2, Rush
5 D1 Coventry A 2-0 Walsh 2
11 D1 Aston V H 2-1 Whelan, Rush
14 D1 Southampton A 1-1 Wark

17 D1 Watford H 4-3 Rush 2, Dalglish, Wark
20 D1 West Ham A 3-0 Walsh 2, Beglin
23 D1 Everton A 0-1
29 ECF Juventus N 0-1

1985/86

Played 57 Won 37 Lost 7 Drawn 13 Goals for 126 Goals against 48
Appearances: Grobbelaar 57, Hansen 56, Rush 54, Johnston, Whelan, Molby 53, Lawrenson 51, Beglin 48, Nicol 41, McMahon 32, Dalglish 29, Walsh 26, Gillespie 22, MacDonald 21, Lee 20, Wark 16, Neal 15, A. Kennedy 8, Seagraves 2.
Scorers: Rush 31, Molby 19, Walsh 16, Whelan 14, McMahon 10, Johnston 9, Wark 6, Dalglish 5, Lawrenson, Nicol 4, Gillespie, MacDonald 3, Beglin, Neal 1.
Total home attendance (29 matches) 952,987. Average 32,861.

August
17 D1 Arsenal H 2-0 Whelan, Nicol
21 D1 Aston V A 2-2 Rush, Molby
24 D1 Newcastle A 0-1
26 D1 Ipswich H 5-0 Nicol, Rush 2, Molby, Johnston
31 D1 West Ham A 2-2 Johnston, Whelan

September
2 D1 N. Forest H 2-0 Whelan 2
7 D1 Watford H 3-1 Neal, Johnston, Rush
14 D1 Oxford A 2-2 Rush, Johnston
20 D1 Everton A 3-2 Dalglish, Rush, McMahon
23 LC Oldham H 3-0 McMahon 2, Rush
28 D1 Spurs H 4-1 Lawrenson, Rush, Molby 2

October
5 D1 QPR A 1-2 Walsh
9 LC Oldham A 5-2 Whelan 2, Wark, Rush, MacDonald
12 D1 Southampton H 1-0 McMahon
19 D1 Man United A 1-1 Johnston
26 D1 Luton H 3-2 Walsh 2, Molby
29 LC Brighton H 4-0 Walsh 3, Dalglish

November
2 D1 Leicester H 1-0 Rush
9 D1 Coventry A 3-0 Beglin, Walsh, Rush
16 D1 West Brom H 4-1 Nicol, Molby, Lawrenson, Walsh
23 D1 Birmingham A 2-0 Rush, Walsh
26 LC Man United H 2-1 Molby 2
30 D1 Chelsea H 1-1 Molby

December
7 D1 Aston V H 3-0 Molby, Walsh, Johnston
14 D1 Arsenal A 0-2
21 D1 Newcastle H 1-1 Nicol
26 D1 Man City A 0-1
28 D1 N. Forest A 1-1 MacDonald

1986/87

January
 1 D1 Sheffield Wed H 2-2 Rush, Walsh
 4 FA Norwich H 5-0 MacDonald, Walsh, McMahon, Whelan, Wark
12 D1 Watford A 3-2 Walsh 2, Rush
18 D1 West Ham H 3-1 Molby, Rush, Walsh
21 LC Ipswich H 3-0 Walsh, Whelan, Rush
26 FA Chelsea A 2-1 Rush, Lawrenson

February
 1 D1 Ipswich A 1-2 Whelan
 9 D1 Man United H 1-1 Wark
12 LCSF QPR A 0-1
15 FA York A 1-1 Molby
18 FA York H 3-1 Wark, Molby, Dalglish
22 D1 Everton H 0-2

March
 2 D1 Spurs A 2-1 Molby, Rush
 4 LCSF QPR H 2-2 McMahon, Johnston
 8 D1 QPR H 4-1 McMahon 2, Rush, Wark
11 FA Watford H 0-0
15 D1 Southampton A 2-1 Wark, Rush
17 FA Watford A 2-1 Molby, Rush
22 D1 Oxford H 6-0 Rush 2, Whelan, Lawrenson, Molby 2
29 D1 Sheffield Wed A 0-0
31 D1 Man City H 2-0 McMahon 2

April
 5 FASF Southampton N 2-0 Rush 2
12 D1 Coventry H 5-0 Whelan 3, Molby, Rush
16 D1 Luton A 1-0 Johnston
19 D1 West Brom A 2-1 Dalglish, Rush
26 D1 Birmingham H 5-0 Rush, Gillespie 3, Molby
30 D1 Leicester A 2-0 Rush, Whelan

May
 3 D1 Chelsea A 1-0 Dalglish
10 FAF Everton N 3-1 Rush 2, Johnston

Played 54 Won 29 Lost 13 Drawn 12 Goals for 97 Goals against 51.
Appearances: Rush 54, Hansen 51, Lawrenson 50, Gillespie 48, McMahon 47, Whelan 46, Molby 44, Grobbelaar 43, Venison 40, Johnston 36, Walsh 31, Beglin 26, Dalglish 23, Nicol 19, Wark 15, Spackman 14, Hooper 11, Aldridge 10, Ablett, MacDonald 6, Irvine 4, Durnin, Mooney 1.
Scorers: Rush 34, McMahon 13, Molby 12, Dalglish 8, Wark 7, Walsh 6, Whelan 5, Nicol 4, Johnston 3, Aldridge, own goals 2, Ablett 1.
Total home attendance (25 matches) 907,125. Average 36,285.

August
23 D1 Newcastle A 2-0 Rush 2
25 D1 Man City H 0-0
30 D1 Arsenal H 2-1 Molby, Rush

September
 3 D1 Leicester A 1-2 Dalglish
 6 D1 West Ham A 5-2 Whelan, Johnston, Dalglish 2, Rush
13 D1 Charlton H 2-0 Molby, Rush
20 D1 Southampton A 1-2 McMahon
23 LC Fulham H 10-0 McMahon 4, Rush 2, Wark 2, Whelan, Nicol
27 D1 Aston V H 3-3 Wark 2, McMahon

October
 3 D1 Wimbledon A 3-1 Molby, Rush 2
 7 LC Fulham A 3-2 McMahon, Parker og, Molby
10 D1 Spurs H 0-1
17 D1 Oxford H 4-0 Rush 2, Dalglish, Molby
24 D1 Luton A 1-4 Molby
29 LC Leicester H 4-1 McMahon 3, Dalglish

November
 1 D1 Norwich H 6-2 Walsh 3, Rush 2, Nicol
 8 D1 QPR A 3-1 Rush, Nicol, Johnston
16 D1 Sheffield Wed. H 1-1 Rush
19 LC Coventry A 0-0
23 D1 Everton A 0-0
26 LC Coventry H 3-1 Molby 3
29 D1 Coventry H 2-0 Molby, Wark

December
 6 D1 Watford A 0-2
14 D1 Chelsea H 3-0 Whelan, Rush, Nicol
20 D1 Charlton A 0-0
26 D1 Man United H 0-1
27 D1 Sheffield Wed. A 1-0 Rush

D1 – League match.   **FA** – FA Cup.   **LC** – League Cup, later Milk Cup and then Littlewoods Cup.   **EC** – European Cup.   **ES** – European Super Cup.   **WC** – World Champions Cup.   **SF** – Semi-final.   **F** – Final.   **A** – Away match.   **H** – Home match.   **N** – Neutral ground.

January
 1 D1 N Forest A 1-1 Rush
 3 D1 West Ham H 1-0 McMahon
11 FA Luton A 0-0
17 D1 Manr C. A 1-0 Rush
21 LC Everton A 1-0 Rush
24 D1 Newcastle H 2-0 Walsh, Rush
26 FA Luton H 0-0
30 FA Luton A 0-3

February
11 LCSF Southampton A 0-0
14 D1 Leicester H 4-3 Walsh, Rush 3
21 D1 Aston V A 2-2 Johnston, Walsh
25 LCSF Southampton H 3-0 Whelan, Dalglish, Molby
28 D1 Southampton H 1-0 Aldridge

March
 7 D1 Luton H 2-0 Molby, Donaghy og
10 D1 Arsenal A 1-0 Rush
14 D1 Oxford A 3-1 Wark 2, Rush
18 D1 QPR H 2-1 Rush 2
22 D1 Spurs A 0-1
28 D1 Wimbledon H 1-2 Dalglish

April
 5 LCF Arsenal N 1-2 Rush
11 D1 Norwich A 1-2 Rush
18 D1 N Forest H 3-0 Dalglish, Whelan, Ablett
20 D1 Man United A 0-1
25 D1 Everton H 3-1 McMahon, Rush 2

May
 2 D1 Coventry A 0-1
 4 D1 Watford H 1-0 Rush
 9 D1 Chelsea A 3-3 Rush, McMahon, Aldridge

1987/88

Played 50 Won 32 Lost 4 Drawn 14 Goals for 99 Goals against 28
Appearances: Nicol 50, Hansen, McMahon 49, Barnes, Beardsley 48, Grobbelaar 46, Aldridge 45, Gillespie 42, Houghton, Johnston 35, Spackman 33, Whelan 31, Ablett, Venison 22, Lawrenson 17, Walsh 9, Molby 8, Hooper 4, Dalglish, Wark 2, MacDonald 1.
Goals: Aldridge 29, Beardsley 18, Barnes 17, McMahon 9, Houghton, Nicol 7, Johnston 6, Gillespie 4, Hansen, Whelan 1.
Total home attendances (23 matches) 905,992. Average 39,390.

August
15 D1 Arsenal A 2-1 Aldridge, Nicol
29 D1 Coventry A 4-1 Nicol 2, Aldridge, Beardsley

September
 5 D1 West Ham A 1-1 Aldridge
12 D1 Oxford H 2-0 Aldridge, Barnes
15 D1 Charlton H 3-2 Aldridge, Hansen, McMahon
20 D1 Newcastle A 4-1 Nicol 3, Aldridge
23 LC Blackburn A 1-1 Nicol
29 D1 Derby H 4-0 Aldridge 3, Beardsley

October
 3 D1 Portsmouth H 4-0 Beardsley, McMahon, Aldridge, Whelan
 6 LC Blackburn H 1-0 Aldridge
17 D1 QPR H 4-0 Johnston, Aldridge, Barnes 2
24 D1 Luton A 1-0 Gillespie
28 LC Everton H 0-1

November
 1 D1 Everton H 2-0 McMahon, Beardsley
 4 D1 Wimbledon A 1-1 Houghton
15 D1 Man United A 1-1 Aldridge
21 D1 Norwich H 0-0
24 D1 Watford H 4-0 McMahon, Houghton, Aldridge, Barnes
28 D1 Spurs A 2-0 McMahon, Johnston

December
 6 D1 Chelsea H 2-1 Aldridge, McMahon
12 D1 Southampton A 2-2 Barnes 2
19 D1 Sheffield Wed H 1-0 Gillespie
26 D1 Oxford A 3-0 Aldridge, Barnes, McMahon
28 D1 Newcastle H 4-0 McMahon, Aldridge 2, Houghton

January
 1 D1 Coventry H 4-0 Beardsley 2, Aldridge, Houghton
 9 FA Stoke A 0-0
12 FA Stoke H 1-0 Beardsley
16 D1 Arsenal H 2-0 Aldridge, Beardsley
23 D1 Charlton A 2-0 Beardsley, Barnes
31 FA Aston V A 2-0 Barnes, Beardsley

February
 6 D1 West Ham H 0-0
13 D1 Watford A 4-1 Beardsley 2, Aldridge, Barnes
21 FA Everton A 1-0 Houghton
27 D1 Portsmouth A 2-0 Barnes 2

March
 5 D1 QPR A 1-0 Barnes
13 FA Man C. A 4-0 Houghton, Beardsley, Johnston, Barnes
16 D1 Derby A 1-1 Johnston
20 D1 Everton A 0-1
26 D1 Wimbledon H 2-1 Aldridge, Barnes

April
 2 D1 N Forest A 1-2 Aldridge
 4 D1 Man United H 3-3 Beardsley, Gillespie, McMahon
 9 FASF N Forest N 2-1 Aldridge 2
13 D1 N Forest H 5-0 Aldridge 2, Houghton, Beardsley, Gillespie
20 D1 Norwich A 0-0
23 D1 Spurs H 1-0 Beardsley

30 D1 Chelsea A 1-1 Barnes

May
2 D1 Southampton H 1-1 Aldridge
7 D1 Sheffield Wed. A 5-1 Johnston 2, Barnes, Beardsley 2
9 D1 Luton H 1-1 Aldridge
14 FAF Wimbledon N 0-1

1988/89

Played 50 Won 31 Lost 7 Drawn 12 Goals for 91 Goals against 40.
Appearances: Nicol 50, Houghton 49, Beardsley, Whelan 48, Ablett 47, Aldridge 46, Barnes 42, McMahon 38, Rush 30, Staunton 28, Grobbelaar 26, Burrows, Hooper 24, Venison 19, Gillespie, Molby 18, Spackman 16, Hansen 8, MacDonald, Watson 5, Dalglish, Durnin, Marsh 1.
Goals: Aldridge 29, Barnes 13, Beardsley 12, Rush 11, Houghton, McMahon 7, Whelan 4, Molby 3, Gillespie, Nicol 2, own goal 1.
Total home attendances (22 matches) 825,317. Average 37,514.

August
27 D1 Charlton A 3-0 Aldridge 3

September
3 D1 Man United H 1-0 Molby
10 D1 Aston V A 1-1 Houghton
17 D1 Spurs H 1-1 Beardsley
24 D1 Southampton A 3-1 Aldridge, Beardsley, Molby
28 LC Walsall H 1-0 Gillespie

October
1 D1 Newcastle H 1-2 Gillespie
8 D1 Luton A 0-1
12 LC Walsall A 3-1 Barnes, Rush, Molby
15 D1 Coventry H 0-0
26 D1 N Forest A 1-2 Rush
29 D1 West Ham A 2-0 Rush, Beardsley

November
2 LC Arsenal H 1-1 Barnes
5 D1 Middlesbrough H 3-0 Rush, Aldridge, Beardsley
9 LC Arsenal A 0-0
12 D1 Millwall H 1-1 Nicol
19 D1 QPR A 1-0 Aldridge
23 LC Arsenal N 2-1 McMahon, Aldridge
26 D1 Wimbledon H 1-1 Houghton
30 LC West Ham A 1-4 Aldridge

December
4 D1 Arsenal A 1-1 Barnes

11 D1 Everton H 1-1 Houghton
17 D1 Norwich H 0-1
26 D1 Derby A 1-0 Rush

January
1 D1 Man Utd A 1-3 Barnes
3 D1 Aston V H 1-0 Whelan
7 FA Carlisle A 3-0 Barnes, McMahon 2
14 D1 Sheffield Wed. A 2-2 Nicol, Aldridge
21 D1 Southampton H 2-0 Aldridge, Rush
29 FA Millwall A 2-0 Aldridge, Rush

February
11 D1 Newcastle A 2-2 Rush, Aldridge
18 FA Hull A 3-2 Barnes, Aldridge 2

March
1 D1 Charlton H 2-0 Beardsley, Aldridge
11 D1 Middlesbrough A 4-0 Beardsley, Houghton, Aldridge, McMahon
14 D1 Luton H 5-0 Aldridge 3, Beardsley, McMahon
18 FA Brentford H 4-0 McMahon, Barnes, Beardsley 2
22 D1 Coventry A 3-1 Barnes, Aldridge, Whelan
26 D1 Spurs A 2-1 Aldridge, Beardsley
29 D1 Derby H 1-0 Barnes

April
1 D1 Norwich A 1-0 Whelan
8 D1 Sheffield Wed. H 5-1 McMahon, Beardsley 2, Houghton, Barnes
11 D1 Millwall A 2-1 Barnes, Aldridge
15 FASF N Forest N Abandoned after six minutes

May
3 D1 Everton A 0-0
7 FASF N. Forest N 3-1 Aldridge 2, Laws og
10 D1 N Forest H 1-0 Aldridge
13 D1 Wimbledon A 2-1 Aldridge, Barnes
16 D1 QPR H 2-0 Aldridge, Whelan
20 FAF Everton N 3-2 Aldridge, Rush 2
23 D1 West Ham H 5-1 Aldridge, Houghton 2, Rush, Barnes
26 D1 Arsenal H 0-2

D1 – League match. **FA** – FA Cup. **LC** – League Cup, later Milk Cup and then Littlewoods Cup. **EC** – European Cup. **ES** – European Super Cup. **WC** – World Champions Cup. **SF** – Semi-final. **F** – Final. **A** – Away match. **H** – Home match. **N** – Neutral ground.

1989/90

Played 49 Won 29 Lost 7 Drawn 13 Goals for 105
Goals against 46
Appearances: Grobbelaar 49, McMahon 48, Rush 47,
Hysen, Whelan 45, Barnes 44, Beardsley 42, Hansen
41, Venison 39, Burrows 36, Staunton 33, Nicol 32,
Ablett 24, Gillespie 19, Molby 14, Rosenthal 9, Tanner
3, Aldridge, Dalglish 1.
Scorers: Barnes 28, Rush 26, Beardsley 15, Nicol 9,
Rosenthal 7, McMahon 6, Gillespie, Staunton 3, Hysen,
Whelan 2, Aldridge, Houghton, Molby, own goal 1.
Total home attendance (24 matches) 857,446.
Average 35,726.

August
19 D1 Man C. H 3-1 Barnes, Beardsley, Nicol
22 D1 Aston V A 1-1 Barnes
26 D1 Luton A 0-0

September
 9 D1 Derby A 3-0 Rush, Barnes, Beardsley
12 D1 C. Palace H 9-0 Nicol 2, McMahon, Rush, Gillespie,
Hysen, Beardsley, Aldridge, Barnes
16 D1 Norwich H 0-0
19 LC Wigan H 5-2 Hysen, Rush 2, Barnes, Beardsley
23 D1 Everton A 3-1 Barnes, Rush 2

October
 3 LC Wigan A 3-0 Staunton 3 (This away leg was played at
Anfield because of safety problems at Wigan)
14 D1 Wimbledon A 2-1 Beardsley, Whelan
21 D1 Southampton A 1-4 Beardsley
25 LC Arsenal A 0-1
29 D1 Spurs H 1-0 Barnes

November
 4 D1 Coventry H 0-1
11 D1 QPR A 2-3 Barnes 2
19 D1 Millwall A 2-1 Rush, Barnes
26 D1 Arsenal H 2-1 McMahon, Barnes
29 D1 Sheffield Wed. A 0-2

December
 2 D1 Manchester C. A 4-1 Rush 2, Beardsley, McMahon
 9 D1 Aston V H 1-1 Beardsley
16 D1 Chelsea A 5-1 Beardsley, Rush 2, Houghton, McMahon
23 D1 Man United H 0-0
27 D1 Sheffield Wed. H 2-1 Molby, Rush
30 D1 Charlton H 1-0 Barnes

January
 1 D1 N. Forest A 2-2 Rush 2
 6 FA Swansea A 0-0
 9 FA Swansea H 8-0 Barnes 2, Whelan, Rush 3, Beardsley, Nicol
13 D1 Luton H 2-2 Barnes, Nicol
20 D1 C Palace A 2-0 Rush, Beardsley
27 FA Norwich A 0-0
30 FA Norwich H 3-1 Nicol, Barnes, Beardsley

February
 3 D1 Everton H 2-1 Barnes, Beardsley
10 D1 Norwich A 0-0
17 FA Southampton H 3-0 Rush, Beardsley, Nicol

March
 3 D1 Millwall H 1-0 Gillespie
11 FA QPR A 2-2 Barnes, Rush
14 FA QPR H 1-0 Beardsley
18 D1 Man United A 2-1 Barnes 2
21 D1 Spurs A 0-1
31 D1 Southampton H 3-2 Barnes, Osman og, Rush

April
 3 D1 Wimbledon H 2-1 Rush, Gillespie
 8 FASF C. Palace N 3-4 Rush, McMahon, Barnes
11 D1 Charlton A 4-0 Rosenthal 3, Barnes
14 D1 N. Forest H 2-2 Rosenthal, McMahon
18 D1 Arsenal A 1-1 Barnes
21 D1 Chelsea H 4-1 Rosenthal, Nicol 2, Rush
28 D1 QPR H 2-1 Rush, Barnes

May
 1 D1 Derby H 1-0 Gillespie
 5 D1 Coventry A 6-1 Rush, Barnes 3, Rosenthal 2

INDEX

Please note that entries in *italics* refer to captions

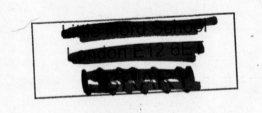